It's another Quality Book from CGP

Want to hear the **bad news**? There's a heck of a lot of
tricky stuff they expect you to learn for KS3 German.

Want to hear the **good news**? Good old CGP have got it all covered.
We've produced this brilliant book with all the words, phrases
and grammar bits clearly laid out and explained.

And then, in the spirit of going the extra mile, we've put some daft bits in to try
and make the whole experience at least vaguely entertaining for you.

We've done all we can — the rest is up to you.

What CGP is all about

Our sole aim here at CGP is to produce the highest quality
books — carefully written, immaculately presented and
dangerously close to being funny.

Then we work our socks off to get them out to you
— at the cheapest possible prices.

Contents

SECTION 6 — PHONE CALLS AND LETTERS

SECTION 7 — WEATHER, HOLIDAYS AND COUNTRIES

SECTION 8 — GRAMMAR AND PHRASES

Published by Coordination Group Publications Ltd.

Editors:

James Paul Wallis
Taissa Csaky

ISBN 1-84146-840-1

Groovy website: www.cgpbooks.co.uk
Jolly bits of clipart from CorelDRAW
Printed by Elanders Hindson, Newcastle upon Tyne.

With thanks to Iryna Csáky and Rachel Thompson for the proofreading.

Numbers

You can't get out of learning <u>numbers</u>. They're just too darned useful.

Learn the numbers — <u>die Zahlen</u>

1 to 10

Go over these numbers <u>again and again</u> till you've got them all <u>memorised</u>. Try counting up to "zehn" on your <u>fingers</u>. When you can do that, count <u>backwards</u> from "zehn" to "eins".

1	2	3	4	5	6	7	8	9	10
eins	zwei	drei	vier	fünf	sechs	sieben	acht	neun	zehn

11 to 20

The words for 13 to 19 all mean "<u>three-ten</u>" etc.
Watch out for 16 and 17 — they're "<u>sechzehn</u>" and "<u>siebzehn</u>".

11	12	13	14	15	16	17	18	19	20
elf	zwölf	dreizehn	vierzehn	fünfzehn	sechzehn	siebzehn	achtzehn	neunzehn	zwanzig

20 to 100

Most "ten-type" numbers are pretty easy — they're "<u>four+zig</u>" (vierzig), "<u>five+zig</u>" (fünfzig) etc.
The odd ones out are "<u>zwanzig</u>", "<u>dreißig</u>", "<u>sechzig</u>" and "<u>siebzig</u>".

20	30	40	50	60	70	80	90	100
zwanzig	dreißig	vierzig	fünfzig	sechzig	siebzig	achtzig	neunzig	hundert

The in-betweens

The in-betweeners are <u>backwards</u> — say "<u>two and twenty</u>", not "twenty-two".

21 einundzwanzig, 22 zweiundzwanzig, 23 dreiundzwanzig, 24 vierundzwanzig...

Add "te" to a number to get <u>fourth, fifth</u> etc...

Just get the number and bung on "<u>te</u>". You need these for saying "<u>third</u> of November", "<u>first</u> on the left" etc.

EXAMPLES:	NUMBER + "te"		
	zwei<u>te</u>	vier<u>te</u>	fünf<u>te</u>
	2nd	4th	5th

1st, 3rd & 7th are a bit different:

erste	dritte	siebte
1st	3rd	7th

When you use these words to describe other words, e.g. "the <u>first</u> bicycle" add <u>r</u> for "der" words, and <u>s</u> for "das" words. See p.60.

For numbers from <u>20</u> to <u>100</u>, add "<u>ste</u>", e.g. zwanzigste, einundreißigste.

Learn your numbers — but don't go in-zehn... (ho ho)

There are no shortcuts here — you just have to say the numbers to yourself <u>over and over again</u>.

Times and Dates

You don't just get to learn numbers — you actually get to use them.
This page is on times and dates. Read, learn, enjoy.

Learn all the clock times

1) THE O'CLOCKS

sieben **Uhr** *seven o'clock*

ein **Uhr** *one o'clock*

Swap this for any number from p.1 for different times.

For one o'clock, you say "ein" (not "eins").

NB — Germans use the 24 hour clock a lot.
4am is 04:00 — *vier Uhr*.
4pm is 16:00 — *sechzehn Uhr*.

2) QUARTER TO and QUARTER PAST

Viertel vor *sieben*
quarter to seven

Viertel nach *sieben*
quarter past seven

You don't need to say "Uhr".

3) MINUTES TO and MINUTES PAST

fünf vor *sieben*
five to seven

fünf nach *sieben*
five past seven

You don't need say "Uhr" for these ones either.

Swap "fünf" for any number you want from p.1

4) HALF ~~PAST~~ TO

halb *sieben*
half to seven
(i.e. half past six)

halb *acht*
half to eight
(i.e. half past seven)

Weird this one — "halb sieben" means half to seven, i.e. half past six. Don't get caught out.

5) AT + TIME

um *sieben Uhr*
at seven o'clock

What time is it? — Wie spät ist es?

THE QUESTION:

Wie viel Uhr ist es? OR *Wie spät ist es?*
What time is it?

THE ANSWER:

Es ist + TIME
It is ......

EXAMPLE:
Es ist drei Uhr.
It's three o'clock.

Other times — today, tomorrow, evening...

Learn these words for chunks of time. They're useful for saying roughly when things happen.

gestern
yesterday

heute
today

morgen
tomorrow

der Tag
day

die Woche
week

der Monat
month

das Jahr
year

das Wochenende
weekend

der Morgen
morning

der Nachmittag
afternoon

der Abend
evening

die Nacht
night

Maybe not today, maybe not tomorrow...

That "half to seven" stuff is weird, but it really is how you do it in German. Have you ever seen *Hunt for Red October*? That had something to do with half-past in it, something about driving a submarine. But nothing to do with German, they were Russians. Even Sean Connery. How does he get away with it?

Times and Dates

More vocab on times and dates.
The days and months aren't <u>too</u> bad — they're not that different to the English names.

Months of the year

Learn them in these <u>groups of four</u>.
They look pretty much like the English months — but look closely at the <u>spellings</u>.

 Januar — January

 Februar — February

 März — March

 April — April

 Mai — May

 Juni — June

 Juli — July

 August — August

 September — September

 Oktober — October

 November — November

 Dezember — December

"It looks to me like the 'P' in April is a little higher off the line."

The days of the week

Seven days, seven bits of vocab...

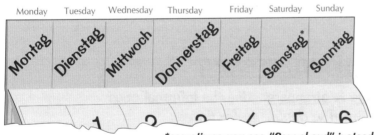

Monday — Montag, Tuesday — Dienstag, Wednesday — Mittwoch, Thursday — Donnerstag, Friday — Freitag, Saturday — Samstag*, Sunday — Sonntag

sometimes you see "Sonnabend" instead

To say, e.g. "on Monday", you put "am" + the day:

Gehen wir am Montag. Let's go <u>on Monday</u>.

To say, e.g. "on Mondays", you put the day with <u>small capital letter</u> and add "<u>s</u>":

Ich schlafe montags. I sleep <u>on Mondays</u>.

Talking about dates

You need dates for <u>booking holidays</u> (p.49) and <u>saying when your birthday is</u> (p.9). Read on...

Start off with "<u>am</u>". Then get the word for "first", "second" etc. from the bottom of p.1 and add "<u>n</u>".
(The "n" is because it's dative, see p.59 if you're interested.)

If you want to do a date that's "<u>20th</u>" or above, don't forget the extra "<u>s</u>":

am neunten April on the ninth of April

am zwölften August on the twelfth of August

am zwanzigsten Mai on the twentieth of May

I like fresh dates, but the dried ones are awful...

Write out the days and months in English and <u>translate</u> them — then translate them back. Do the same with them in a <u>random</u> order — this'll make sure you really know <u>each</u> of 'em, not just the list.

Meeting and Greeting

Off the top of my head I can think of <u>two</u> songs about "<u>hello</u>" and "<u>goodbye</u>"
(1. The Beatles, 2. David Gray). Don't listen to them — just <u>learn the German</u>.

Saying hello — Guten Tag

The first thing you'll hear or say is one of these <u>greetings</u>.
Learn these ice-breakers and when to use which one.

1) There are <u>two general ones</u>:

> **Guten Tag**
> *Hello*

Quite <u>formal</u>. Literally means 'good day'.

> **Hallo**
> *Hi*

Less formal, i.e. you'd say it to your <u>mates</u>.

2) There are also specific hello words for <u>different times</u> of the day:

> **Guten Morgen**
> *Good morning*

> **Guten Tag**
> *Good day*

> **Guten Abend**
> *Good evening*

> **Gute Nacht**
> *Good night*

3) You can say hello words either on their own, or with a <u>name</u>.
E.g. *Guten Morgen, Daniela / Guten Tag, Herr Schröder / Hallo Thomas* etc...

Saying goodbye — Auf Wiedersehen

You want a <u>formal goodbye</u> for <u>older people</u> & <u>strangers</u>. Use the <u>informal</u> ones
for your <u>mates</u> or people your <u>own age</u>. But *if in doubt, go for formal*.

> **Auf Wiedersehen**
> *Goodbye*

This is a bit <u>formal</u> — it literally means 'until we see each other again'.

> **Tschüss**
> *Bye*

Both of these are <u>more casual</u>.

> **Bis später**
> *See you later*

Auf Wiedersehen, pet...

So <u>that's</u> what it means. "Goodbye, pet". "Pet" is northeast slang for "dear". They were off to
Germany. To be builders. And they said goodbye to their families. *...He was better in <u>Morse</u>.*

Meeting and Greeting

Lots more useful phrases for when you first <u>meet</u> people... Manners cost nothing etc.

May I introduce ██ — <u>Darf ich ██ vorstellen?</u>

Sometimes you might have to <u>introduce</u> someone. Here's how:

Darf ich Ihnen Stefan vorstellen?
May I introduce Stefan?

Swap "<u>Ihnen</u>" for "<u>dir</u>" if you're speaking to someone your age or younger.

Swap "<u>Ihnen</u>" for "<u>euch</u>" if you're speaking to more than one person your age or younger.

Here's <u>another way</u> of saying it.

Darf ich Ihnen meinen Freund vorstellen? Er heißt Stefan.
May I introduce my friend? He's called Stefan.

If you're introducing a girl or woman, say "meine Freund<u>in</u>", and "<u>sie</u> heißt".

Pleased to meet you

When <u>you've</u> been introduced, reply with "pleased to meet you".

Schön, dich kennen zu lernen. *Pleased to meet you.* ⬅ Informal version.

Schön, Sie kennen zu lernen. *Pleased to meet you.* ⬅ Formal version.

How are you? — <u>Wie geht es dir?</u>

If your mate's dog just died it'd be best to <u>find out</u>, <u>before</u> you start rabbitting on about how happy <u>you</u> are and how brilliant your life is. <u>**Learn how to say "How are you?"**</u>

These phrases all mean '<u>How are you?</u>':

1) **Wie geht es dir?**

2) **Wie geht's?** People say this a lot to their friends. It's a <u>short</u> version of 1).

3) **Wie geht es Ihnen?** This is the <u>formal</u> version.

Swiss Science #317: invention of the weather house.

All very <u>similar</u> ways of saying pretty much the same thing. **Take your pick...**

Here's what you could <u>answer</u>: **Gut, danke.** *I'm well, thanks.*

<u>Greet vb. Scottish weep; cry – origin OE, partly from ḡretan...</u>*

In England you normally say "This is Kevin," everybody says "Alright Kevin," and that's it. German-speakers are that little bit <u>more formal</u>, so you need all this manners-type vocab off pat.

*At least that's what my dictionary said.

Being Polite

OI, YOU, LEARN THIS. (Irony, eh — what a *great* invention that was.)

Please and thank you — *bitte, danke*

You don't want to go round <u>winding people up</u> — learn how to say please and thank you.

bitte	*danke*	*danke schön*
please	thank you / thanks	thank you very much

Yes, no — *ja, nein*

If somebody asks you if you want something you could just answer with "yes" or "no":

ja	*nein*
yes	no

But obviously it's loads <u>better</u> to say "Yes, please," or "No, thank you."

Ja, bitte.	*Nein, danke.*
Yes, please.	No, thanks.

You're welcome — *bitte schön*

You hear this <u>everywhere</u>. Shop assistants probably say it about a thousand times a day.

Sometimes people just say "bitte". → *bitte schön* / you're welcome

Get yourself off the hook — say *sorry* and *excuse me*

Learn this <u>phrase</u> for "I'm sorry":

es tut mir Leid

Es tut mir Leid, aber ich mag nicht Käse.
I'm sorry, but I don't like cheese.

This is how you say "<u>excuse me</u>" politely:

entschuldigen Sie

Entschuldigen Sie, wo ist das Kino bitte?
Excuse me, where is the cinema please?

A grateful contortionist — bitte and twisted...

The top three sections are the basic <u>must-have</u> bits of German. If you learn <u>nothing else</u>, learn those words and how to <u>spell</u> them. Then practise adding "<u>bitte</u>" and "<u>danke</u>" to your sentences to make them polite.

Being Polite

It's the same in any language — saying "I want chips" doesn't work, but "Could I have a bag of chips, please?" works wonders. This page is about saying "I would like" not "I want".

I would like... — Ich möchte...

1) "I would like" (ich möchte) is polite, "I want" (ich will) is dead rude:

 Ich will Käse.
I want some cheese.   <u>NO!</u> Rude as rude can be.

 Ich möchte Käse.
I would like some cheese.   <u>Much better</u>. There'll be cheese coming at you from all sides.

*Swiss Science #318:
the cheese hole.*

2) You can also say you'd like <u>to do</u> something:

Ich möchte + VERB

Ich möchte <u>singen</u>. I would like <u>to sing</u>.
Ich möchte Fußball <u>spielen</u>. I would like <u>to play</u> football.
Ich möchte <u>ausgehen</u>. I would like <u>to go out</u>.

The verb has to be in the <u>infinitive</u> form — see p.63.

May I...? — Darf ich...?

Be polite by <u>asking permission</u> to do things.
This is the special <u>rule</u> for saying 'May I...?':

Haben and singen are
<u>infinitives</u> — see p.63.

Darf ich + INFINITIVE

Darf ich ein Brötchen <u>haben</u>, bitte?
May I have a roll, please?

Darf ich <u>singen</u>, bitte?
May I sing, please?

Offer to help, and don't upset people

1) Ask if you can <u>help</u> — it makes you look good. (See p.15 for more chores.)

	das Essen vorbereiten?	*May I...*	*prepare the meal?*
Darf ich...	*den Tisch decken?*		*lay the table?*
	spülen?		*do the washing up?*

2) If you're going to say something you think <u>they won't like</u>, start with "es tut mir Leid":

Es tut mir Leid, aber ich esse kein Fleisch.
I'm sorry, but I don't eat meat.

I would like one million pounds and a private jet...

Remember "want" = <u>BAD</u>, "I would like" = <u>GOOD</u>. There are tons of variations for the "I would like" and "May I" sentences — learn all the examples here, and write out <u>at least five</u> more of your own.

Summary Questions

There can only be one lucky winner, and tonight the winner is YOU. Your prize is a fabulous sun-soaked adventure in the tropical Maldives, basking on the white sand, diving amongst schools of glittering fish, and lazily snorkelling across the turquoise waters of the coral reef — and as a special bonus we've thrown in 22 KS3 German questions. Enjoy. (I'm really sorry but I lied about the holiday.)

1) Count to ten in German, out loud preferably.

2) Count backwards from ten to one in German.

3) Count to twenty in German — out loud.

4) Write down the German for these numbers: *(in words, not numbers — I'm not a complete sucker)*
   a) 23   b) 32   c) 37   d) 73   e) 100

5) Write down your house number in German.

6) Write down the number of people in your German class in German.

7) Translate these words into German, and write them out in words:
   a) first   b) third   c) seventh   d) ninth

8) Write out all these times in German, in words:
   a) 09:00   b) 10:10   c) 11:15   d) 12:40   e) 13:30   f) 14:45

9) Translate this fascinating conversation:
   "Wie viel Uhr ist es?"   "Es ist Viertel vor fünf."

10) Answer this question in German:
    "Wie spät ist es?"

11) Put these time words in size-order, with the one that lasts longest first:
    der Tag   das Jahr   der Monat   die Woche

12) Write down "der", "die" or "das" for each of these words:
    Morgen   Nachmittag   Abend   Nacht

13) What's today called in German?

14) Which of these phrases would you be likely to use with people your own age?
    a) Guten Tag   b) Hallo   c) Auf Wiedersehen   d) Tschüss

15) What time of day would it be if somebody said "Guten Abend" to you?

16) You're out in town with your German penfriend and you run into someone she knows. She says: *"Darf ich dir Clothilde vorstellen?"* What does it mean?

17) How do you say "Pleased to meet you," in German?

18) Write down three different ways of saying "How are you?" in German.

19) How do you say "Yes, please" and "No, thanks"?

20) You've accidentally trodden on the Chancellor's grandma's ingrowing toenail. What do you say?

21) Which of these sounds more polite?
    "Ich möchte Elefanten."   or   *"Ich will Elefanten."*

22) Write this out in German.
    "Can I wash the car?"

Your Details

Old joke: "Me, me, me, me, me. Anyway, I've talked enough about me — what do you think of me?"

① Talking about yourself — facts and figures

You need to know these <u>four questions</u>, and how to <u>answer</u> them.
Customise the answers to fit <u>you</u>, by changing the <u>underlined</u> bits.

Which one's Sheila?

THE QUESTIONS:	THE ANSWERS:
What are you called? **Wie heißt du?**	**Ich heiße <u>Sheila</u>.** I'm called <u>Sheila</u>.
How old are you? **Wie alt bist du?**	**Ich bin <u>vierzehn</u> Jahre alt.** I'm <u>fourteen</u>.
When is your birthday? **Wann hast du Geburtstag?**	**Ich habe am <u>vierten Juli</u> Geburtstag.** My birthday is <u>4th July</u>.
What do you like? **Was magst du?**	**Ich mag <u>Schokolade</u>.** I like <u>chocolate</u>.

For more numbers and dates, see p.1-3.

For other ways of saying what you like and don't like see p. 53.

② Say what you look like

<u>Eyes</u>, <u>hair</u>, <u>height</u>, <u>glasses</u> — GO GO GO:

EYES

Ich habe <u>grüne</u> Augen. I have green eyes.

green: **grüne**   blue: **blaue**   brown: **braune**

HEIGHT

Ich bin <u>klein</u>. I am short.

small: **klein**   fat: **dick**
tall: **groß**   thin: **dünn**
medium height:
mittelgroß

HAIR

Ich habe <u>blonde</u> Haare. I have blonde hair.

blonde: **blonde**   short: **kurze**
black: **schwarze**   shoulder-length: **schulterlange**
brown: **braune**   quite long: **relativ lange**
red: **rote**

GLASSES

I wear glasses:
Ich trage eine Brille.
I don't wear glasses:
Ich trage keine Brille.

③ Describe your personality

Ich bin...
I am...

| **fleißig** hardworking | **sportlich** sporty | **nett** nice |
| **faul** lazy | **schüchtern** shy | |

fig 9.1: Sporty Austrians. Strangely disturbing.

If you're a sheep, just talk about ewe...

It's all great stuff for a <u>first letter</u> to a <u>penpal</u>. If your hair's a <u>weird colour</u> like green, there are more colours on p.32. Make sure you learn the <u>birthday</u> bit, or there's no way of dropping hints. <u>No hints</u> = <u>no cake</u>.

Your Family

A lot of these German words <u>sound</u> a bit like the English. Try stuffing plums in your mouth, then saying the words out loud. Remember: <u>plums</u> + <u>English</u> = <u>German</u>.

Use these words for your *friends* and *family*

mein Vater
my father

meine Mutter
my mother

STEP STUFF

mein Stiefvater
my stepfather

meine Stiefmutter
my stepmother

mein Stiefbruder
my stepbrother

meine Stiefschwester
my stepsister

mein Freund
my friend (male)

meine Freundin
my friend (female)

mein Bruder
my brother

meine Schwester
my sister

mein Großvater
my grandfather

meine Großmutter
my grandmother

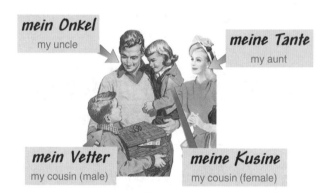

mein Onkel
my uncle

meine Tante
my aunt

mein Vetter
my cousin (male)

meine Kusine
my cousin (female)

Say what your *family* and *friends* are *like*

Use these phrases to describe your <u>friends</u> and <u>family</u> (swap Bruder/Schwester for anything you want).
The phrases are slightly <u>different</u> for <u>lads</u> or <u>lasses</u> (see those underlined bits) so I've written them out twice.

PHRASES ABOUT LADS

I have a brother. = *Ich habe <u>einen</u> Bruder.*

<u>*Mein* Bruder heißt John.</u>
= My brother is called John.

He's eleven years old. = <u>*Er*</u> *ist elf Jahre alt.*

He's nice. = <u>*Er*</u> *ist nett.*

PHRASES ABOUT LASSES

Ich habe <u>eine</u> Schwester. = I have a sister.

<u>*Meine* Schwester heißt Louise.</u>
= My sister is called Louise.

<u>*Sie*</u> *ist elf Jahre alt.* = She's eleven years old.

<u>*Sie*</u> *ist nett.* = She's nice.

If you're an only child, say
<u>*"Ich bin ein Einzelkind"*</u> = I am an only child.

Spot the chestnuts...

Alright, <u>test yourself</u> — write this out in German: *"I have an aunt. My aunt is called Heidi. She's thirty-five years old. She's nice"*. The answer's on p.18 — if you didn't get it 100% right, <u>try again</u>.

Pets and Animals

If you don't have a pet, you *could* just pretend you do. It might be a lie, but it'll help you learn German.

Learn the pets — die Haustiere

Don't just learn each animal name, learn if it's der, die or das as well.

der Vogel
bird

das Pferd
horse

die Kuh
cow

grrr

der Hund
dog

das Kaninchen
rabbit

die Katze
cat

der Hamster
hamster

die Maus
mouse

die Schildkröte
tortoise

I have a hamster — Ich habe einen Hamster

You need to understand people talking about their pets, and talk about yours if you have one.
I've used "Hamster" as an example — swap in the animal word for the pet you want to talk about.

1) **Ich habe** **einen Hamster** . = I have a hamster.

It's "einen" for "der" animals, but "eine" for "die" ones,
and "ein" for "das" ones (see p.58).

2) **Mein Hamster** **heißt "Killer"**. = My hamster is called "Killer".

It's "mein" for "der" animals, but "meine" for "die"
ones, and "mein" for "das" ones (see p.56).

3) **Ich habe keine Haustiere.**
= I don't have a pet.

4)
Mein Hamster **ist**
My hamster is

süß sweet
böse nasty
groß big
schwarz black

My dog's got no nose. How does it smell? Awful...

Just thinking about point 4) over there on the right... If you want to go into more fascinating detail
about your pet, see: p.9 for "small"; p.32 for other colours; p.9 for personality types. Great.

Your Home

What a corker, eh. <u>Rooms</u> come up all <u>over the place</u>. Furniture's a bit more specialised, but you still need it.

Talk about the <u>rooms</u> in your house — *die Zimmer*

['das Zimmer' = room]

das Wohnzimmer	das Schlafzimmer	das Badezimmer	die Küche	das Esszimmer	der Garten
living room	bedroom	bathroom	kitchen	dining room	garden

At home — *zu Hause*

THE QUESTION:

Was für ein Haus hast du? = *What's your house like?*

"Zu Hause gibt es fünfhundert Zimmer."

THE ANSWERS:

<u>Change</u> the <u>underlined</u> bits so they match <u>your</u> home.
See p.1 for more numbers.

Zu Hause gibt es <u>fünf</u> Zimmer.   **OR**   **Zu Hause gibt es <u>eine Küche und zwei Schlafzimmer</u>.**

= *In my home, there are <u>five</u> rooms.*   = *In my home, there is <u>a kitchen and two bedrooms</u>.*

The bit after "es gibt/ gibt es" is accusative, so it's <u>einen</u> for "der" words, <u>eine</u> for "die", and <u>ein</u> for "das" words (see p.58).

Talk about the <u>furniture</u> — *die Möbel*

das Bett	das Sofa	der Stuhl	der Tisch	der Schrank	der Kleiderschrank
bed	sofa	chair	table	cupboard	wardrobe

In your room — *In deinem Schlafzimmer*

Learn this <u>question</u>, and how to <u>answer</u> it. <u>Change</u> the <u>underlined bit</u> to make it match <u>your</u> room — choose from the furniture above. And remember — <u>einen</u> for "der", <u>ein</u> for "das" words, and <u>eine</u> for "die" words.

THE QUESTION:

Was für Möbel gibt es in deinem Schlafzimmer?

= *What furniture is there in your bedroom?*

THE ANSWERS:

Es gibt <u>ein Bett und ein Stuhl</u>.

= *There is a bed and a chair.*

Sofa so good...

See the pics of rooms at the top? Use them to <u>test</u> if you've <u>learnt</u> the vocab — use strips of paper to <u>cover up</u> the German, then from the pictures, write down the German names for the rooms.

Where You Live

This is describing <u>whereabouts</u> your home is. It's all good <u>Key Stage Three German</u> stuff...

Tell them where you live — *Ich wohne...*

① Say if you live in a <u>flat</u> or a <u>house</u>...

Ich wohne in...
Ich lebe in...
I live in...

...einer Wohnung
...a flat

...einem Haus
...a house

② ...and if you live in a <u>village</u>, <u>town</u> or <u>city</u>.

EXTRA ONES

Ich wohne in...   I live in...

...einem Dorf   *...einer Stadt*   *...einer Großstadt*
...a village   ...a town   ...a big town / city

Ich lebe auf dem Land.
I live in the countryside.

Ich wohne in den Bergen.
I live in the mountains.

Ich wohne am Meer.
I live at the seaside.

③ Work out the version of this phrase that <u>you</u> need, and learn it <u>off by heart</u>.

I live in <u>Oxford</u>, <u>a town</u> in <u>the south of England</u>.

Ich wohne in Oxford , einer Stadt in Südengland .

Put the <u>name</u> of where you live in here.

einem Dorf
a village

einer Stadt
a town

einer Großstadt
a big town/city

Choose the right <u>compass bit</u> from the right. Then add on your country, to make one big word.

Schottland
Scotland

Wales
Wales

Nordirland
Northern Ireland

COMPASS DIRECTIONS

Nord north
Nordwest northwest   *Nordost* northeast
West west   *Ost* east
Südwest southwest   *Südost* southeast
Süd south

Do you like living here? — *Lebst du gern hier?*

Saying <u>what you think</u> about where you live is just what you need to get your German to a <u>higher level</u>.

Ich lebe gern hier
I like living here

...weil es fantastich *ist.* ...because it's <u>fantastic</u>.

interessant interesting   *ruhig* quiet

Ich lebe nicht gern hier
I don't like living here

...weil es furchtbar *ist.* ...because it's <u>terrible</u>.

langweilig boring   *zu ruhig* too quiet

Ich lebe "gern" hier — nothing to do with pulling faces...

Presumably, at least someone in your class lives in the <u>same place</u> as you. You should get the <u>same thing</u> for the sentence in number 3. Work it out for yourself with this page, then check with someone else. If you wrote <u>different</u> things, something's gone Pete Tong — ask teach.

Daily Routine

Here's a page about <u>daily routine</u>. It's got <u>daily routine</u> on it. If you want <u>daily routine</u>, this is <u>your page</u>...

Daily routine — say what you do

You need to know <u>all these bits</u>. Take them one at a time, read them carefully and check out the <u>spellings</u>.

Ich wache auf.
I wake up.

Ich stehe auf.
I get up.

Ich wasche mich.
I wash myself.

Ich putze mir die Zähne.
I brush my teeth.

Ich ziehe mich an.
I get dressed.

Ich esse Frühstück.
I eat breakfast.

Ich gehe zu Fuß zur Schule.
I walk to school.

(See p.20 for "by bus", "by car" etc.)

Ich gehe nach Hause.
I go home.

Ich mache meine Hausaufgaben.
I do my homework.

Ich sehe fern.
I watch telly.

Ich esse Abendessen.
I eat dinner.

Ich gehe ins Bett.
I go to bed.

Homework, hmm — great...

You're in luck — you can check you've got it all sussed by <u>covering up</u> the words with a piece of paper, and next to each picture write out the <u>German phrase</u> to go with it. Then check you got them <u>all right</u>. If you didn't, read through it all, then <u>try again.</u> Keep going till you get them <u>all</u>.

Chores

Chores a-plenty, yessiree. For some reason, you have to talk about what chores you do at home. This stuff is good for offering to help as well (see p.7).

Learn the nine chores

Not that "doing nothing" really counts as a chore. Pity.

Machst du Hausarbeit?
Do you do any housework?

I wash the dishes.

Ich spüle.

I clean.

Ich putze.

I do the vacuum cleaning.

Ich sauge Staub.

I make my bed.

Ich mache mein Bett.

I don't do anything.

Ich mache nichts.

I tidy my room.

Ich räume mein Zimmer auf.

I wash the car.

Ich wasche das Auto.

I lay the table.

Ich decke den Tisch.

I go shopping.

Ich gehe einkaufen.

Housework, hmm — fab...

Well, it could be worse. You could have to get the water from a well at the top of the hill, and scrape the fire clean with a badger. Or whatever they did in the old days.

The Body

You need <u>body parts</u> for a) telling people <u>something hurts</u> (next page),
b) telling the police something nasty's washed up on the beach.

The head — der Kopf

the nose **die Nase**

the mouth **der Mund**

the tooth **der Zahn**
the teeth **die Zähne**

das Auge the eye

das Ohr the ear

die Haare hair

The body — der Körper

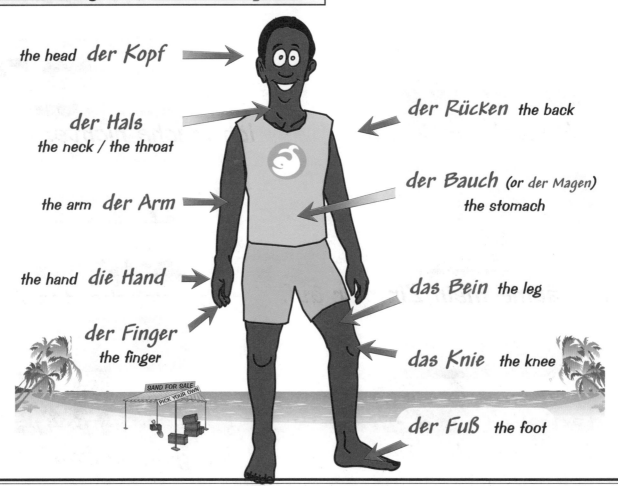

the head **der Kopf**

der Hals
the neck / the throat

the arm **der Arm**

the hand **die Hand**

der Finger
the finger

der Rücken the back

der Bauch (or **der Magen**)
the stomach

das Bein the leg

das Knie the knee

der Fuß the foot

SAND FOR SALE
PICK YOUR OWN

Get your foot off my tip box...

Come on, some of these <u>aren't hard</u> at all — like die <u>Hand</u>, der <u>Finger</u>, der <u>Arm</u>. You're halfway there
without even trying. And joy of joys, you can do the trick of <u>covering the labels</u> with some paper,
and writing out the German for all the body bits <u>from memory</u>. If you miss any, <u>try again</u>. Chin up.

Health and Illness

Being ill <u>sucks</u>. Don't suffer in silence, learn this German and get <u>made better</u> **ASAP**. Cough, wheeze.

Say that you're ill — "Ich bin krank"

Ich bin krank.
I am ill.

Say where you want
to go to get better:

Ich will ins Krankenhaus gehen.
I want to go <u>to the hospital</u>.

Ich will zum Arzt gehen.
I want to go <u>to the doctor's</u>.

Ich will zur Apotheke gehen.
I want to go <u>to the pharmacy</u>.

My leg hurts — Mein Bein tut mir weh

This is how you say what bit of you <u>hurts</u>. Practise bunging in the <u>body parts</u> from page 16.

"mein / meine" + BODY PART + "tut mir weh"

Mein Bein tut mir weh.
My leg hurts

*It's "mein" for "der" and "das" words,
and "meine" for "die" words.
See p.56 for more.*

EXAMPLES

Mein Fuß tut mir weh. My foot hurts.

Meine Hand tut mir weh. My hand hurts.

Meine Nase tut mir weh. My nose hurts.

Mein Kopf tut mir weh. My head hurts.

For your <u>head</u>, <u>stomach</u> and <u>ear</u>, you can say they hurt,
or you can use the special "<u>ache</u>" words, like this:

Ich habe <u>Kopfschmerzen</u>. *I have a <u>headache</u>.*

Ich habe <u>Bauchschmerzen</u>. *I have <u>stomachache</u>.*

Ich habe <u>Ohrenschmerzen</u>. *I have <u>earache</u>.*

Learn these things for making you better

If you're ill, you'll need one of these things to <u>make you better</u>. Get them <u>learned</u>.

die Medizin
= medicine

die Salbe
= ointment

das Rezept
= prescription

das Pflaster
= plaster

die Tablette
= tablet

die Schmerztablette
= painkiller

Enough German — let's have some astronauts...

*Did you know, real
live German people
have been in space?
They certainly have:*

*German payload
specialists Ernst
Messerschmid
and Reinhard Furrer,
13/12/84*

*Image of
Oberpfaffenhofen
in Germany.*

*German and
American
astronauts on a
joint mission.*

Summary Questions

I bet you thought there wasn't going to be any fun in this book. How wrong you were. This page is packed full of fun, laughter and joy. If you really love answering German questions, that is. Look back through the section to help yourself answer the questions until you're sure you've got them all right. Then try the questions again without looking back. You can't say you know the stuff unless you can answer the whole lot without looking, peeping or otherwise taking shortcuts.

1) How do you ask a friend what their name is in German?

2) Write this conversation out in German:
   "When's your birthday?" "It's on the fifth of March."

3) Describe yourself in German. Mention your height, the colour of your eyes and the colour of your hair.

4) Which one of these sentences means "I'm lazy"?
   a) Ich bin fleißig.   b) Ich bin faul.

5) Write down the names of everyone in your family, then write down the German phrases for what relation they are to you.

6) Say you've got one brother. Say he's called Finbar and he's ninety-five years old.

7) Write this sentence out in German:
   "I've got a horse, a bird, a tortoise and a hamster."

8) Write "My horse is nasty," in German.

9) Write three headings — <u>der</u>, <u>die</u> and <u>das</u>. Write each of these words under the right heading:

Schrank	Stuhl	Garten	Sofa
Küche	Schlafzimmer	Badezimmer	Esszimmer
Bett	Kleiderschrank	Tisch	Wohnzimmer

10) Now write down what all the words from question 9) mean.

11) Answer this question in German: *Was für Möbel gibt es in deinem Wohnzimmer?*

12) What does this mean in English: *Ich wohne in einer Großstadt.*

13) Write these out in German:
    a) eastern England   b) western Wales   c) southern Scotland   d) northern Northern Ireland

14) Say *"I like living here because it's quiet."* (Now say it like you mean it.)

15) Put these sentences about daily routine into a sensible order, then translate them into English:
    Ich wasche mich.   Ich gehe ins Bett.   Ich wache auf.   Ich esse Abendessen.
    Ich esse Frühstuck.   Ich gehe in die Schule.   Ich ziehe mich an.   Ich gehe nach Hause.

16) Write down *"I lay the table."* and *"I tidy my room."* in German.

17) What do *"Ich wasche das Auto."* and *"Ich sauge Staub."* mean in English?

18) Write a German label for each arrow on this picture. Don't forget to put <u>der</u>, <u>die</u> or <u>das</u>.

19) Write this out in German:
    I'm ill. My head hurts. I want to go to the hospital.

20) What do these three words mean?
    die Salbe   das Rezept   die Schmerztablette

Answer to page 10: *Ich habe eine Tante. Meine Tante heißt Heidi. Sie ist fünfunddreißig Jahre alt. Sie ist nett.*

Section 2 — You, Family and Home

School Subjects

School — it's a funny old place really. All <u>teachers</u> and <u>pupils</u> and <u>lessons</u>.
Now, <u>beaches</u> — they're more <u>sandy</u>, with <u>sea</u> all down one side. Yep, school <u>isn't</u> the beach.

School subjects — *die Schulfächer*

Learn <u>all</u> these subjects so you can say what you do. Tackle them <u>one group at a time</u>.

SCIENCE

die Naturwissenschaft — science
die Physik — physics
die Chemie — chemistry
die Biologie — biology

NUMBERS & STUFF

die Mathe(matik) — maths
die Informatik — IT

HUMANITIES

die Geschichte — history
die Erdkunde / die Geografie — geography
die Reli(gion) — religious studies

PHYSICAL EDUCATION

der Sport — PE

ART & MUSIC

die Kunst — art
die Musik — music

LANGUAGES

das Englisch — English
das Deutsch — German
das Französisch — French
das Spanisch — Spanish

Say <u>what you do</u>. It's just "<u>ich lerne</u>" + subject:

> **Ich lerne <u>Deutsch</u>.** *I study German.*

My favourite subject — *mein Lieblingsfach*

Raise your German level a ton by <u>giving opinions</u> about your subjects. For more on opinions see p.53.

SUBJECT + "ist mein Lieblingsfach" → **Musik ist mein Lieblingsfach.** *Music is my favourite subject.*

 Ich mag Geschichte. *I like history.*   **Ich hasse Geschichte.** *I hate history.*

Remember, it's "er" for "der" words, "sie" for "die" words, "es" for "das" words (see p.57).

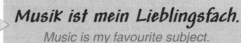 **...weil er/sie/es einfach ist.** *...because it's easy.*

interesting: interessant   easy: einfach   useful: nützlich
boring: langweilig   difficult: schwierig   pointless: nutzlos

We don't need no education — oh yes you do...

You need to learn all <u>16 subjects</u>, even the ones you <u>don't</u> do. There are <u>9 opinion phrases</u> — write a <u>different</u> opinion for each of the 9 subjects from Science, Numbers & Stuff and Humanities.

School Routine

If <u>aliens</u> invade, speaking German and asking about your <u>typical school day</u>, you're gonna <u>need</u> this stuff or they'll eat your <u>brains</u> on toast. *...Or, learn it 'cos you need it for <u>KS3 German</u>.* Your choice.

The school day — *der Schultag*

Go through these phrases, and <u>write out</u> your own version of each one so it matches <u>your</u> day.

| *Ich fahre mit dem*
I go by | *Auto* car
Bus bus
Fahrrad bike | *zur Schule.*
to school | *For more on transport, see p.40-41.* |

For more on transport, see p.40-41.

BUT... *Ich gehe zu Fuß zur Schule.* I go to school on foot.

For more on home routine, see p.14.

For more on times, see p.2.

Ich stehe um acht Uhr auf. I get up at 8:00.

Die Schule fängt um neun Uhr an. School begins at 9:00.

Die Schule ist um vier Uhr aus. School ends at 4:00.

Jede Stunde dauert vierzig Minuten. Each lesson lasts forty minutes.

Wir haben acht Stunden pro Tag. We have eight lessons per day.

For more on numbers, see p.1.

Wir machen eine Stunde Hausaufgaben pro Tag.
We do one hour of homework every day.

"Stuff homework. Go skiing"

School days — the happiest days of your life, or so they say...

It's all good practice of <u>numbers</u> and <u>times</u>, which you can use <u>all over the place</u>. Even for interesting stuff like arranging when to have fun. I was at a restaurant with some mates last night. We met up <u>at 6:30</u>. That'd be "<u>um halb sieben</u>". Anyway. With all these phrases watch out for the <u>spellings</u> — <u>don't</u> mix up your "an" with your "aus". Even the <u>tiny words</u> have to be <u>right</u>.

Classroom Stuff

If your teacher is anything like mine was, they'll <u>talk to you in German</u>. Learn this page to have a fighting chance. If they're shouting "Seid ruhig!" and you're yapping like a good'un, you'll be for it.

In the classroom — *im Klassenzimmer*

When you're in German class, <u>use</u> the German words for the <u>classroom objects</u>.
Even if you just say "Where's my Kuli?" it'll help lodge the German words in your head.

das Buch
book

das Übungsheft
exercise book

der Bleistift
pencil

der Kuli / der Kugelschreiber
pen

das Lineal
ruler

der Radiergummi / Gummi
rubber

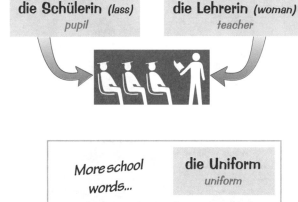

der Schüler *(lad)*
die Schülerin *(lass)*
pupil

der Lehrer *(bloke)*
die Lehrerin *(woman)*
teacher

More school words...

die Uniform
uniform

die Stunde
lesson

der Stundenplan
timetable

Sit down! — *Setzt euch!*

Like I say, you need these <u>memorised</u>, or you could do something daft when teach uses them.

Steht auf!   = Stand up!

Hört zu!   = Listen!

richtig   = true

Setzt euch!   = Sit down!

Seid ruhig!   = Be quiet!

falsch   = false

Use these phrases if you get <u>a bit stuck</u>

Was bedeutet das?   = What does that mean?

Wie sagt man das auf Deutsch?   = How do you say that in German?

Wie sagt man das auf Englisch?   = How do you say that in English?

Sit down, be quiet and eat your dog biscuits...

Not sure what that means. Move on. Remember "Buch" is for proper <u>printed books</u>, and "Übungsheft" is for <u>exercise books</u> you write in — it's the kind of thing teachers get het up about.

Jobs

There are different words for job titles depending on whether it's a man or a woman doing the job.
The "♂" words are for men, the "♀" ones are for women.

Here are the jobs — die Berufe

('der Beruf' = job)

WORDS ENDING WITH "in" FOR WOMEN

♂ *Mechaniker*
♀ *Mechanikerin*
mechanic

♂ *Bauarbeiter*
♀ *Bauarbeiterin*
builder

Affix photo of your favourite teacher here.

♂ *Lehrer*
♀ *Lehrerin*
teacher

♂ *Verkäufer*
♀ *Verkäuferin*
salesperson

♂ *Schauspieler*
♀ *Schauspielerin*
actor/actress

♂ *Ingenieur*
♀ *Ingenieurin*
engineer

♂ *Sekretär*
♀ *Sekretärin*
secretary

♂ *Polizist*
♀ *Polizistin*
policeman/woman

♂ *Arzt*
♀ *Ärztin*
doctor

♂ *Zahnarzt*
♀ *Zahnärztin*
dentist

WORDS WITH DIFFERENT ENDINGS

♂ *Friseur*
♀ *Friseuse*
hairdresser

♂ *Krankenpfleger*
♀ *Krankenschwester*
nurse

♂ *Büroangestellter*
♀ *Büroangestellte*
office worker

Hairdressers who do frizzy hair are called frizzeurs...

It's a pain learning two words for every job. Mainly the words for women are the same as they are for men, but with '-in' stuck on the end. You'll have to triple-learn the odd ones like "Friseuse".

Talking About Jobs

In the old days, you'd finish school and be working up a chimney by now. Nowadays you have a few more options. Learn this German, and if you don't know what you want to do, just pretend.

Tell 'em what you want to do — Ich möchte...

Use this sentence for what you want to study (for GCSE's or A-levels or whatever):

"Ich möchte" + SUBJECT + "lernen"

Ich möchte Biologie lernen... I want to study biology

See p.19 for more subjects.

Give a short reason why:

...weil es interessant ist. because it's interesting

...weil es einfach ist. because it's easy

...weil es lustig ist. because it's fun

...weil ich Arzt werden möchte. because I want to be a doctor

Talk about jobs like this:

"Ich möchte" + JOB + "werden"

Ich möchte Arzt werden

I want to become a doctor

You can use any of the reasons from above, or this one:

...weil sie viel Geld verdienen.

...because they earn a lot of money.

Say what you do and other people do

Work out and practise saying what you do (if you have a job), and what your parents do. For other people, swap 'mein Vater' with e.g. 'mein Bruder' or 'meine Freundin Liz' (see p.10).

Ich bin Polizist.
I am a policeman.

Meine Mutter ist Polizistin.
My mother is a policewoman.

Mein Vater ist Polizist.
My father is a policeman.

REMEMBER: Don't put 'ein' or 'eine'. Just put 'bin' or 'ist' and the job.

Which one's Mum?

If you've got a part-time job, say what it is, or where you work:

Ich habe einen Teilzeitjob. I have a part-time job.

Ich trage Zeitungen aus.
I deliver newspapers.

Ich arbeite bei Kwik Save.
I work at Kwik Save.

When I grow up I'm going to be taller...

For about the next five years adults (teachers mainly) will be endlessly asking what you want to do with your life. German teachers are no different, so for minimum hassle get this stuff learned.

Summary Questions

You've rearranged all the pens on your desk. You've looked out the window for a bit. You've had a little think about what you're going to do at the weekend. But still these darned questions are staring up at you. They're not going to go away. Answer all the questions — look back through the section for help at first, but aim to be able to answer every single one without looking back.

1) Write a German sentence starting "Ich lerne..." for every subject you do.

2) Write "Ich mag..." and "Ich hasse..." sentences for each of the subjects you wrote down for question 1.

3) Write a sentence using each of these words for three of the subjects from Q1:
   a) nutzlos   b) langweilig   c) schwierig

4) How do you get to school? Answer in German.

5) What time do you normally get up? Answer in German.

6) How long is each of your lessons? Answer in German.

7) How much homework do you have to do each day? Answer in German.

8) What kind of book is "das Buch"? What kind of book is "das Übungsheft"?

9) Write three headings — "der", "die" and "das",
   then copy these words out under the right headings.

Lehrer	Schülerin	Stundenplan	Kuli
Buch	Lehrerin	Übungsheft	Bleistift	Uniform
Lineal	Schüler	Gummi	Stunde

10) Write the English meaning next to each of the words from Q9.

11) If somebody says "Steht auf!" what do they want you to do?

12) What could you say in German to find out what a German word means? Write down two ways of saying it.

13) Write down what each of these words means and put F by the ones used for women, and M by the ones used for men.

Mechanikerin	Bauarbeiter	Lehrerin	Verkäuferin	Schauspieler
Ingenieur	Sekretärin	Polizistin	Ärztin	Zahnarzt

14) Write in German:
   "I want to study history because it's interesting. I want to be an actor because it's fun."

15) Write two more sets of sentences like the ones in Q.14. Write one about what you really want to do and one about the worst subject and job you can possibly imagine. Use a dictionary if you can't find the vocab.

16) What does "Meine Mutter is Ärztin" mean in English?

17) Write down sentences to say what jobs everyone in your family does.

Directions

One thing you <u>always</u> have to do in German lessons is use a dodgy map to give directions to the person sitting next to you. Even if you never go to Germany, you need to <u>learn</u> this stuff.

Where is ░░? — Wo ist ░░?

Step 1 — Asking the Way

You need to learn <u>both</u> these phrases for "Where's the..." so you can <u>understand</u> and <u>use</u> them. *I've used "das Kino" for the example — swap it for any place you like (see p.26 and 27 for other places).*

Wo ist <u>das Kino</u>, bitte?
Where is the <u>cinema</u>, please?

Gibt es hier in der Nähe <u>ein Kino</u>?
Is there a cinema near here?

Step 2 — Giving Directions

gehen Sie links
go left

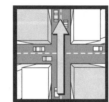

gehen Sie geradeaus
go straight on

gehen Sie rechts
turn right

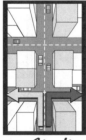

nehmen Sie die erste Straße *links*/rechts
take the first street *on the left*/on the right

nehmen Sie die zweite Straße *links*/rechts
take the second street *on the left*/on the right

"And next week children we'll learn about left."

Distances — say if it's near or far

You don't just want to know <u>where</u> you're going. You'll need to find out <u>how far</u> it is too.

QUESTION
Wie weit ist es von hier? How far is it from here?

Change "zwei" to any number (see p.1).

ANSWER
Es ist <u>weit</u> von hier.
It's <u>far</u> from here.

ANSWER
Es ist <u>in der Nähe von</u> hier.
It's <u>near</u> here.

ANSWER
Es ist <u>zwei</u> Kilometer von hier.
It's <u>two</u> kilometres from here.

Where am I??? — oh, it's alright, I'm over here...

Once, in Berlin, I was walking to the shops, when a family with <u>seven</u> little kids came up and asked me the way to the zoo, all talking at once. Boy was I glad I'd done KS3 German. Oh yes.

SHOPS

Many legacies of Roman rule endure in the ancient province of Germania.
Outstanding amongst these are the vine, the excellent transport network and a multitude of shops.

THE SHOPS: DIE GESCHÄFTE

("DAS GESCHÄFT" = SHOP)

das Süßwarengeschäft
sweet shop

die Bäckerei
bakery

die Konditorei
cake shop

der Markt
market

die Metzgerei
butcher's

die Buchhandlung
bookshop

der Lebensmittelladen
grocer's

die Apotheke
pharmacist's

die Drogerie
general chemist's

der Supermarkt
supermarket

So what have the Romans ever done for us...

Just ten bits of shopping vocab. But don't go thinking you can take it easy. Fewer bits to learn means you can learn each one extra well. That means spellings 100% right, from memory. Oh yes, indeedy. As Caesar said to Brutus.

Section 4 – Town, Shopping, Food and Drink

Places in Town

Places to go, things to see. Some of these are a doddle — they're exactly the <u>same</u> as they are in English. Look out for "das Theat<u>er</u>" though — the 'r' and the 'e' have been sneakily swapped around.

17 Places to Learn

das Museum
museum

das Freizeitzentrum
leisure centre

das Rathaus
town hall

der Bahnhof
train station

die Bibliothek
library

die Bank
bank

der Park
park

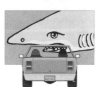
das Kino
cinema

das Theater
theatre

die Stadtmitte
town centre

die Post
post office

das Schloss
castle

das Hotel
hotel

das Schwimmbad
swimming pool

das Krankenhaus
hospital

die Kirche
church

das Verkehrsbüro
tourist information

And one for luck... die Scholle *plaice*

You never know, you might want to go to one of these places. In the big park in Munich people <u>surf</u> on a weir and <u>sunbathe</u> in the buff. It's true. I've seen it with my own eyes. Shocking, eh.

Food and Drink

On the plus side there are <u>no phrases</u> to learn on this page. On the down side it's all vocab. <u>Enjoy</u>.

Meat — das Fleisch

das Schweinefleisch
pork

das Lammfleisch
lamb

das Steak
steak

die Wurst
sausage

der Fisch
fish

das Hähnchen
chicken

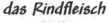

das Rindfleisch
beef

der Schinken
ham

die Meeresfrüchte
seafood

Fruit — das Obst

der Apfel
apple

die Birne
pear

die Orange
orange

die Zitrone
lemon

der Pfirsich
peach

die Erdbeere
strawberry

die Banane
banana

Vegetables — das Gemüse

die Tomate
tomato

die Karotte
carrot

der Kohl
cabbage

der Kopfsalat
lettuce

der Blumenkohl
cauliflower

die Erbsen
peas

der Pilz
mushroom

die Kartoffel
potato

die Zwiebel
onion

Yes, that really was the Chancellor's name...

You'll always get a good feed in Germany. Unless you don't know any food vocab of course.
Learn it all. Learn what's <u>der</u>, <u>die</u> and <u>das</u>. Copying things out helps loads. You know the drill.

Food and Drink

Right, time for some serious concentration — some of the most important vocab
in this book is <u>right here</u> on this page. In fact, it's <u>2.9 cm</u> from this full stop.

Sweet things — die Süßigkeiten

Learn these words about delicious, sweet, <u>sugary</u> things.

 die Marmelade jam

 die Schokolade chocolate

 der Keks biscuit

 der Zucker sugar

 das Eis ice cream

 der Kuchen cake

Dairy Gubbins

die Milch milk   **die Sahne** cream   **der Joghurt** yoghurt
der Käse cheese   **die Butter** butter

 das Ei egg

Other stuff — mainly stodge

The last few bits of food vocab...

 das Brot bread

 die Nudeln pasta

 die Getreideflocken cereal

 *der Reis* rice

 *die Pommes frites* chips

 die Kartoffelchips crisps

And Some Lovely Drinks — die Getränke

Cold'uns

 die Cola cola

 das Mineralwasser mineral water

 der Orangensaft orange juice

 der Weißwein white wine

 der Rotwein red wine

 das Bier beer

Hot'uns

 der Tee tea

 die heiße Schokolade hot chocolate

 der Kaffee coffee

Kind of a drink

 die Suppe soup

It's not all sausages you know...

...I mean, there are lots of sausages in Germany, never mind Austria and Switzerland.
But there are other things too, like ham, and salami, and roast pork, and <u>pig knuckles</u>. Mmmm.

Food and Drink

Like food? Love eating? You're in luck — there's a whole page of talking about food. Pig out.

I like... — Ich mag...

These "like" / "don't like" phrases come up all over the place, get them learned.

Ich mag Orangen **.**   = I like oranges.

rice: Reis
bananas: Bananen

See p.53 for more on opinions.

Ich mag Orangen **nicht.**   = I don't like oranges.

peas: Erbsen
cream: Sahne

See p.28-29 for names of foods.

I'm hungry — Ich habe Hunger...

The normal German phrase for "I'm hungry" is "Ich habe Hunger" — literally, "I have hunger."

Hast du Hunger?
Are you hungry?

Ja, ich habe Hunger.
Yes, I am hungry.

Nein, ich habe keinen Hunger.
No, I am not hungry.

Hast du Durst?
Are you thirsty?

Ja, ich habe Durst.
Yes, I am thirsty.

Nein, ich habe keinen Durst.
No, I am not thirsty.

Say what you eat

 Ich esse **Wurst** *.* I eat sausage.

 Ich trinke **Wasser** *.* I drink water.

Say when you eat

das Frühstück
breakfast

das Mittagessen
lunch

das Abendessen
evening meal

MEALTIMES

Das Frühstück ist um acht Uhr.   Breakfast is at 8 o'clock.

Das Mittagessen ist um halb ein.   Lunch is at half past twelve.

Das Abendessen ist um sieben Uhr.   The evening meal is at 7 o'clock.

See p.2 for clock times.

If you eat up everything on your plate...

OK, this page is packed. Don't get your undercrackers in a twist, just take it one chunk at a time.

Food and Drink

A few <u>restaurant odds and bobs</u>, then the real meat — <u>restaurant conversations</u>.
Err, that proves I've read the page, now it's, err, your turn. Hmm. Restaurants are a
<u>key topic</u> for <u>KS3 German</u>, and dead useful for holidays. <u>That's</u> why this stuff is here.

Restaurant Vocab

"das Restaurant" should be pretty easy to remember...

das Restaurant
restaurant

der Kellner
waiter

die Kellnerin
waitress

das Getränk
drink

die Speisekarte
menu

die Vorspeise
starter

das Hauptgericht
main course

der Nachtisch
dessert

Restaurant Conversations

Get yourself a table, order what you want to eat and drink, and pay at the end:

1) Get yourself a <u>table</u>:

Einen Tisch für <u>zwei</u> Personen, bitte.   A table for <u>two</u>, please.

Stick any number from p.1 here. One person is "eine Person".

2) The waiter/waitress asks <u>what you want</u>:

Was möchten Sie?   What would you like?

Ich hätte gern <u>Fisch</u>.   I would like <u>fish</u>.

More food and drink
words on p.28-29.

Etwas zu trinken?   Anything to drink?

Ich nehme eine <u>Cola</u>.   I'll have a <u>cola</u>.

*"Grilled or
poached, sir?"*

3) At the end of the meal, <u>say you'd like to pay</u>:

Zahlen, bitte.   I'd like to pay, please.

...You'll get a really nasty lollipop...

"<u>Ich hätte gern</u>..." is a great phrase to learn — you can use it <u>whenever</u> and <u>wherever</u> you want
something, and sound dead polite too. *e.g. "Ich hätte gern ein Auto" = I would like a car.*

Clothes and Colours

Two pages of hiding your nakedness. The <u>basics</u> on <u>this page</u>, then how to <u>buy stuff</u> on the <u>next</u>. <u>Enjoy</u>.

Learn your clothing — *die Kleidung*

There's a lot to learn here. <u>Break it down</u> into <u>chunks</u> of say 4 items, and learn 'em a chunk at a time.

das Hemd
man's shirt

die Bluse
woman's shirt

das T-Shirt
T-shirt (no kidding)

der Pullover
jumper

die Hose
trousers

die Jeans
jeans

das Kleid
dress

der Rock
skirt

der Mantel
coat

der Regenmantel
raincoat

die Jacke
jacket

der Hut
hat

die Socke / die Socken
sock / socks

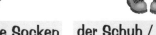
der Schuh / die Schuhe
shoe / shoes

der Handschuh / die Handschuhe
glove / gloves

die Brille
glasses

Say What You Wear

"Ich trage" + "einen / eine / ein" + GARMENT

Ich trage ein T-shirt.
I'm wearing a T-shirt.

It's "<u>einen</u>" for "<u>der</u>" things, "<u>eine</u>" for "<u>die</u>" things, "<u>ein</u>" for "<u>das</u>" things. See p.56.

Colours **and** Materials

Yep, colours and materials — what more can I say...

schwarz *black*	**grau** *grey*	**weiß** *white*	**rot** *red*	**gelb** *yellow*

	grün *green*	**blau** *blue*	**rosa** *pink*	**orange** *orange*	**braun** *brown*	

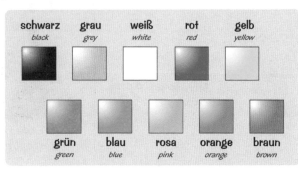
die Wolle
wool

die Baumwolle
cotton

das Leder
leather

E.G.
der weiße Rock the white skirt

To be 100% correct you have to stick an ending on the colour word — see p.60.

Add a material to a garment to make one giant word. (But drop the "e" from *Wolle* and *Baumwolle*.) ➞ *ein Wollpullover*
a woollen jumper

School Uniform

And now for the truly fashion-conscious...

*Ich trage eine graue Hose,
einen Wollpullover,
eine schwarze Krawatte,
und ein Baumwollhemd.*

I wear grey trousers, a woollen sweater, a black tie and a cotton shirt.

Clothes and Colours

How can you <u>shop</u> without <u>words</u>... and how can you <u>live</u> without <u>shopping</u>...

Asking for stuff — ich möchte...

① **Ich möchte _einen Rock_.**
   I would like _a skirt_.

   OR

   Ich hätte gern _einen Rock_?
   I would like _a skirt_?

   Stick "bitte" on the end of these to make them more polite.

② **Sonst noch etwas?**
   Anything else?

   OR

   Sonst noch einen Wunsch?
   Anything else?

   ✓ **Ja, bitte.**
   Yes, please.

   OR

   ✗ **Nein, danke.**
   No, thank you.

Sonst noch etwas?
Nein, danke.

③ ✓ **Ich nehme das.**
   I'll take that one.

   OR

   ✗ **Ich lasse es.**
   I'll leave it.

Asking How Much Things Cost

Was kostet das?
How much is that?

Das kostet zwei Euro.
It costs two euros.

OR

Zwei Euro.
Two euros.

German money — it's euros now

In 2002, Germany changed over to the <u>euro</u>. So did most of Europe. How convenient.
Lucky for you it's pretty easy — there are <u>100 cents</u> in a <u>euro</u>, like there are 100 pence in a pound.

This is what you'd <u>see</u> on a German <u>price tag</u>.
They use a <u>comma</u>, not a decimal point:

€ 5,50

This is the euro symbol.

Some euro odds and bobs.

This is how you <u>say</u> the price: **"Fünf Euro fünfzig Cent"**

A unified pan-European currency — EUROnly a referendum away...

OK, you've got to learn <u>all</u> this stuff, but here are some specific things to do: 1) Complete the sentence "<u>I'm wearing a</u> ..." for each thing you're wearing now. 2) Write out a paragraph to say what your <u>school uniform</u> is. 3) Write out a <u>conversation</u> where you go to buy a <u>jacket</u>.

Summary Questions

Whoopee-doo, more questions to test what you know... The horrible truth is that they are <u>not</u> fun, but they <u>are</u> the only way to find out whether you really know your stuff. If you don't absorb a bit of information from this book then one thousandth of a tree will have died in vain, so think of the trees and do these questions till you can get all the answers right without looking back through the book (or over your mate's shoulder).

1) Ask where the museum is in German.

2) Translate this into English:
   "Gehen Sie geradeaus. Nehmen Sie die zweite Straße links, und dann die erste Straße links.

3) Ask how far away the museum is and translate this answer: *"Es ist sechshundert Meter von hier."*

4) Write down two German "der" names for shops, two "die" names, and one "das" one.

5) Sort these words out into three columns headed "der", "die" and "das":

Theater	Bibliothek	Verkehrsamt	Rathaus
Kino	Stadtmitte	Postamt	Schwimmbad
Kirche	Hotel	Bahnhof	Park

6) Now translate all the words from Q5) into English.

7) Write down the German names of six different types of meat.

8) Make a list, in German, of fruit and vegetables you like.

9) Make a list, in German, of fruit and vegetables you don't like.

10) Translate this shopping list into English:

Meeresfrüchte	Tomaten	Brot	Erdbeeren
Rindfleisch	Kopfsalat	Käse	Sahne
Kartoffeln	Zwiebeln	Schokolade	Zucker

11) There's one mistake in each of these words for drinks. Copy them out and correct the mistakes.

   die Supe   die Kola   der Weisswein   die Tee   der Koffee   der Orangnsaft

12) How do you say "I'm hungry" in German? How do you say "I'm not thirsty?"

13) Write down the German for "I eat meat. I drink orange juice."

14) Translate this into English:
   Das Frühstück ist um Viertel nach acht. Das Mittagessen ist um dreizehn Uhr.
   Das Abendessen ist um zwanzig Uhr.

15) Write down the German for starter, main course and pudding including the "der", "die" or "das".

16) What's this in English?
   Was möchten Sie? Ich hätte gern Lammfleisch.

17) How do you ask for the bill in German?

18) Make a list of things you normally wear at the weekend (in German), including the colours and materials.

19) You want to buy a loaf of bread. The shopkeeper says "Das kostet drei Euro." How much is it?

Sports and Musical Instruments

Sports and instruments, hot dang. All the sports and instruments you need for KS3 German are here, and how to say you play them. Learn 'em all, and make double-sure you know the ones you play. Let the games commence.

Talk about sport — *der Sport*

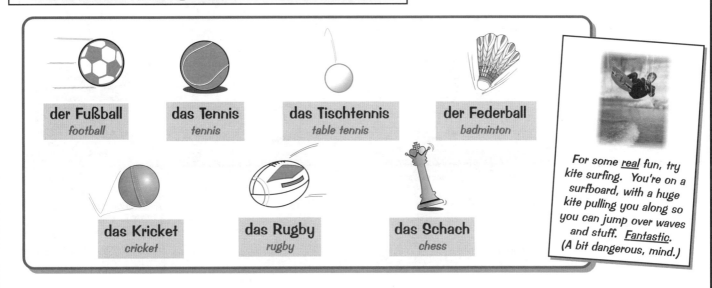

der Fußball
football

das Tennis
tennis

das Tischtennis
table tennis

der Federball
badminton

das Kricket
cricket

das Rugby
rugby

das Schach
chess

For some real fun, try kite surfing. You're on a surfboard, with a huge kite pulling you along so you can jump over waves and stuff. Fantastic. (A bit dangerous, mind.)

Learn the instruments — *die Instrumente*

[das Instrument = instrument]

die Trompete
trumpet

die Klarinette
clarinet

die Querflöte
flute

das Klavier
piano

die Trommeln
drums

die Geige
violin

die Gitarre
guitar

das Cello
cello

How To Say What You Play...

"Ich spiele" + THING

Ich spiele Fußball. I play football.

EXAMPLES:
Ich spiele Tennis. I play tennis. **Ich spiele Gitarre.** I play the guitar.

Learning German — it's all fun and games...

Try this for the sports bit: get two strips of paper to cover up the grey boxes. Then on the paper, write down the German for each sport. Keep doing it till you can get them all right from memory.

Pastimes and Hobbies

Would ya Adam and Eve it. More <u>pastimes</u> here, these are ones you <u>do</u> rather than play.
The <u>opinion</u> stuff at the bottom is a <u>beauty</u>. ...Well, it's <u>dead useful</u> at least.

What do you do in your free time?

Was machst du in deiner Freizeit?

Ich gehe wandern
I go hiking

Ich gehe schwimmen
I go swimming

Ich fahre Rad
I cycle

Never mind that lot, try ultimate frisbee. It's <u>brilliant</u>. Two teams of 7, and you catch a frisbee in the "end zone" to score. Check out www.ukultimate.com

Ich gehe Kegeln
I go bowling

Ich gehe Schlittschuh laufen
I go ice-skating

Ich gehe einkaufen
I go shopping

Say what you do and don't like

Talk about your <u>opinions</u>, and have your teacher choking on their Hobnob in delight. You need this stuff to show your German's worth the <u>top levels</u>. Good thing is, it's pretty <u>easy</u>. Ish.

Magst du Tennis? Do you like tennis?

Ich mag Tennis.
I like tennis.

↓

Ich liebe Tennis.
I love tennis.

↓

...weil es* interessant **ist.** *...because it's interesting.*

(einfach) easy (lustig) fun

Ich mag Tennis nicht.
I don't like tennis.

↓

Ich hasse Tennis.
I hate tennis.

↓

...weil es* langweilig **ist.** *...because it's boring.*

(schwierig) difficult (ermüdend) tiring

*It's <u>er</u> for <u>der</u> words, <u>sie</u> for <u>die</u> words, <u>es</u> for <u>das</u> words. See p.57.

Be careful how you spell "Schlittschuh"...

<u>Hate</u> sports, shopping, and generally anything that involves standing up? You still have to learn this page, so you can say <u>why</u> you don't like doing stuff. Sorry. *...Actually I'm not sorry, get off your rear, lazy.*

TV, Books and Radio

Put down your ice-axe and pick up the <u>remote control</u>. This page is more relaxing.

I listen to the radio — *Ich höre Radio*

Ich höre Radio. *= I listen to the radio.*

Musik *music*

Ich höre Radio gern.
I like to listen to the radio.

Ich höre Radio nicht gern.
I don't like to listen to the radio.

I read books — *Ich lese Bücher*

Ich lese Bücher. *= I read books*

Zeitungen *newspapers*
Romane *novels*
Zeitschriften *magazines*

Ich lese Bücher gern.
I like to read books.

Ich lese Bücher nicht gern.
I don't like to read books.

I watch television — *Ich sehe fern*

Ich sehe fern. *= I watch TV*

Ich sehe Filme an. *= I watch films*

Ich sehe gern fern.
I like to watch TV

Ich sehe nicht gern fern.
I don't like to watch TV

I like this film — *Ich mag diesen Film*

Ich mag ... / Ich mag ... nicht
I like / I don't like

diesen Film this film
diese Musik this music
diese Zeitung this newspaper

diesen Roman this novel
diese Zeitschrift this magazine

EXAMPLES: Ich mag diesen Film. *I like this film.*   Ich mag diesen Film nicht. *I don't like this film.*

Most people look best on the radio...

Ahh, that's better. Words to describe couch-potatoing. But where's the vocab for big woolly socks, a sofa, take-away pizza, and a <u>big box of chocolates</u>? Sorry, turned into Bridget Jones there.

Going Out and Making Arrangements

Classic KS3 German stuff on this double page spread. Learn <u>all 4 steps</u> so you can get from <u>hanging around</u> on your <u>own</u>, to <u>having fun</u> out with your <u>mates</u>. (Assuming your mates speak German...)

Step ① — Places to Go

These are the main <u>places</u> you'd want to go to. They're the places I'd want to go anyway. For other places, see p.26-27.

die Stadtmitte
town centre

das Schwimmbad
swimming pool

das Kino
cinema

das Theater
theatre

das Freizeitzentrum
leisure centre

das Restaurant
restaurant

zu Hause
home

Step ② — Do you want to...

Use this phrase with one of the places above.

Hast du Lust + | *in den* / *in die* / *ins* | **PLACE + zu gehen ?**

Hast du Lust ins Kino zu gehen?
Do you want to go to the cinema?

It's "in die" for "die" words, "in den" for "der" words and "ins" for "das" words.

"<u>Zu Hause</u>" is the <u>odd one out</u>. You <u>don't</u> put "ins zu Hause" — you say "<u>nach Hause zu gehen</u>".

"YES" PHRASES

Ja, gerne. Yes, I'd like to.

Ja, das wäre schön. Yes, I'd love to.

Ja, gute Idee. Yes, good idea.

"NO" PHRASES

Nein, danke. No, thank you.

Ich gehe nicht gern ins Kino. I don't like going to the cinema.

Ich habe kein Geld. I don't have any money.

Ich mache meine Hausaufgaben. I'm doing my homework.

Hast du Lust ins "Museum of Soil" zu gehen — nein, danke...

Life's too short — just learn the phrases for "yes" and get out there.

Going Out and Making Arrangements

Step ③ — Say When and Where to Meet

When shall we meet? — "Wann treffen wir uns?"

Be specific...

Treffen wir uns *Let's meet*

um zwanzig Uhr	at eight o'clock (pm)
um elf Uhr	at eleven o'clock (am)

You can stick any clock times in here — see p.2.

...or be vague.

Treffen wir uns *Let's meet*

heute abend this evening	
morgen tomorrow	
morgen früh tomorrow morning	
am Donnerstag on Thursday	

For other days of the week, see p.3.

Where shall we meet? — "Wo treffen wir uns?"

Treffen wir uns *Let's meet*

in der Stadt in town	
im Restaurant in the restaurant	
bei mir zu Hause at my house	

When you're meeting in a place say "im" for "der" and "das" words, and "in der" for "die" words.

There's a new word here — "<u>vor</u>", which means "in front of".

Treffen wir uns *Let's meet*

vor dem Schwimmbad in front of the swimming pool	
vor dem Kino in front of the cinema	

Here you need "dem" for "der" and "das" words, and "der" for "die" words. See p. 59.

Step ④ — Buying Tickets

If you don't have a <u>ticket</u>, they won't let you in.

 Was kostet eine Karte, bitte? *How much does a ticket cost?*

Eine Karte kostet zehn Euro. *A ticket costs ten euros.*

 **Ich möchte** *I would like*

eine Karte one ticket	
zwei Karten two tickets	
drei Karten three tickets	

bitte. *please.*

INSERT GAG HERE

Look back over <u>both</u> these pages, and make sure you can put <u>all</u> the phrases <u>together</u>.
<u>Test yourself</u> by putting this lot into <u>German</u>: *"Let's go to the town centre. Yes, I'd love to. When shall we meet? Let's meet at 7 o'clock. Where shall we meet? Let's meet in front of the theatre."*

Transport

This is all wonderful stuff to use in Germany — should help you get on the <u>tram</u> to the <u>zoo</u>, not the <u>train</u> to <u>Moscow</u>. You can use it to talk about how you get around at home too.

das Auto
car

der Bus
bus

der Reisebus
coach

das Fahrrad
bicycle

das Motorrad
motorbike

der Zug
train

die U-Bahn
underground

die Straßenbahn
tram

das Schiff
ship

das Flugzeug
aeroplane

All aboard the KS3 German Fun-Train...

It's dead easy this page — just <u>ten</u> bits of vocab to learn, and of course remembering which ones are "der", "die" and "das". I'd love to stick around and help but I've got a train to catch...

That really is Benz and Mercedes. Karl Benz, and Mercedes Jellinek. He made cars, she was the daughter of an Austrian businessman who sold them (he sold Daimler cars, but Daimler merged with Benz in 1926).

Transport

My Mum had a foreign penfriend back in the 60's. He was on the run from Interpol, because he didn't want to join the army. He escaped by skiing through Finland at night. <u>Ignore that</u>, <u>read this</u>:

I go by... — Ich fahre mit...

Dead useful this. It comes up when you're talking about <u>going out</u>, <u>going to school</u> and <u>holidays</u>.

> **"Ich fahre mit dem/der" + VEHICLE**
>
> **Ich fahre mit dem Auto.** *I go by car.*

Note for Swots
It's <u>mit dem</u> for "der" and "das" words, and <u>mit der</u> for "die" words (see p.59).

Use it for <u>any</u> of the transport types from p.40.
Here are the <u>three other most common</u> ones:

> **Ich fahre mit dem Zug** *I go by train*
> **Ich fahre mit dem Bus** *I go by bus*
> **Ich fahre mit dem Fahrrad** *I go by bike*

There's a special phrase
for <u>going on foot</u>:

> **Ich gehe zu Fuß.** *I go on foot.*

Use the same phrases for train and bus tickets

Germany has good trains that <u>actually work</u>, if you can imagine that.
There are quite a few phrases to learn here, but it's <u>essential stuff</u> for buying tickets.

Fährt <u>ein Zug</u> nach Berlin? *Is there a train going to Berlin?*

For a bus, change it to "<u>ein Bus</u>" or "<u>der Bus</u>".

For more times, see p.2

Q: Wann fährt <u>der Zug</u> nach Berlin? *When does the train for Berlin leave?*
A: Der Zug nach Berlin fährt um neun Uhr. *The train for Berlin leaves at nine o'clock.*

Steamy picture no.1

Q: Von welchem Gleis fährt <u>der Zug</u> nach Berlin? *Which platform does the train for Berlin leave from?*

A: Der Zug nach Berlin fährt von Gleis drei. *The train for Berlin leaves from platform three.*

Q: Was für eine Fahrkarte brauchen Sie? *What kind of ticket do you need?*
A: Eine einfache Fahrkarte nach Berlin, erste Klasse, bitte. *A single to Berlin, 1st class, please.*

eine einfache Fahrkarte
a single ticket

eine Rückfahrkarte
a return ticket

1st erste Klasse
first class

2nd zweite Klasse
second class

Steamy picture no.2

This ticket's been used, I want to return it...

Make sure you've got it sussed — <u>test yourself</u> by rewriting this <u>in German</u> (answer on p.42):
"Is there a train to München? I would like a return, first class. When does the train leave?"

Summary Questions

So now you're all ready to go out and kick some conversational ass at the chess clubs of Köln, and the railway stations of Regensburg. My, the fun you're going to have. Before you get on the internet to book your tickets make sure you know the stuff by doing the questions. All the questions. Till you get them all right without trying. How many times do I have to say it... How many times do I have to say it... How many times...

1) Write down the German for each of these:
   a) rugby   b) table tennis   c) cricket   d) football   e) badminton   f) tennis
   Don't forget the "der", "die" and "das" — it's too easy otherwise.

2) What are these called in English?
   a) die Gitarre   b) das Klavier   c) die Querflöte   d) die Trommeln   e) die Geige

3) Write out three German sentences starting "Ich spiele" about sports or instruments from p.35 and p.36.

4) How do you say these in German?
   a) I cycle.   b) I go bowling.   c) I go shopping.   d) I go hiking.   e) I go ice-skating.

5) Write a German sentence using "Ich _____ gern" or "Ich _____ nicht gern" about each of these:
   a) cricket   b) listening to the radio   c) watching TV   d) going shopping   e) going ice-skating

6) What does this question mean in English?
   Hast du Lust ins Theater zu gehen?

7) What does this question mean in English?
   Hast du Lust ins Freizeitzentrum zu gehen?

8) What's wrong with this question?
   Hast du Lust ins Hause zu gehen?

9) Your German exchange partner's good-looking cousin asks whether you want to go to the town centre. Write down three different ways of saying 'yes'.

10) Your German exchange partner's creepy-looking cousin asks whether you want to go to a restaurant. You <u>definitely</u> don't want to go. Say no politely, and make an excuse.

11) The gorgeous cousin asks you a question. What does it mean?
   Um wie viel Uhr treffen wir uns?

12) Write down this answer in German: "Let's meet tomorrow morning."

13) The cousin says: *Treffen wir uns bei mir zu Hause.* Where are you going to meet?

14) While you're in town you decide to go and see a film. Eager to show off your linguistic talent you ask for two tickets. What would you say, in German?

15) Sort these words out into three columns, "der", "die" and "das".
   Auto   Bus   Flugzeug   Fahrrad   Motorrad
   Reisebus   Schiff   Straßenbahn   U-Bahn   Zug

16) Write down what all the words from Q15) mean in English.

17) Write three sentences starting "Ich fahre mit dem / der ..." for each of these types of transport,
   a) underground   b) coach   c) car

18) How do you ask if there's a train going to Budapest, in German?

19) How do you ask which platform the train leaves from?

20) Ask for a return ticket, second class, to Fleissheim.

Answer to p.41: Fährt ein Zug nach München? Eine Rückfahrkarte, erste Klasse, bitte. Wann fährt der Zug?

Telephones and Post Office

Learn this, or get stuck in Austria eating Zunge, with no way to tell anyone to come get you. Be warned.

Telephone numbers — *die Telefonnummer*

die Telefonnummer telephone number

Say your phone number in groups of 2, e.g. thirty-five, not three five (see p.1 for numbers):

Meine Telefonnummer ist fünfunddreißig, vierzig, zweiundzwanzig.

My telephone number is 35, 40, 22.

Here's what you say when you phone someone:

 Hallo! Hier spricht Ben. Hello, it's Ben here.

Kann ich mit Kaspar sprechen? Can I speak to Kaspar, please?

At the post office — *Auf der Post*

der Brief letter

der Briefumschlag envelope

 die Postkarte postcard

die Briefmarke stamp

die Adresse address

der Briefkasten postbox

München, den 1. April 2002

Liebe Katrina

heute ...

Ulrich Mannschmidt
Krebsochstr. 24
890545 München

Katrina Feldheim
Albrechtstr. 32
890527 München

This is how you ask for a stamp:

 Ich möchte eine Zwei-Euro-Briefmarke, bitte.
I'd like a two-euro stamp.

eine Ein-Euro-Briefmarke
a one-euro stamp

If you don't know what kind of stamp you need, this is what to say:

 Ich möchte einen Brief nach Großbritannien schicken. Was kostet es?
I'd like to send a letter to Britain. How much is that?

Obviously you can change 'Großbritannien' to whatever country you need, e.g. Frankreich. 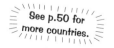 See p.50 for more countries.

Oh Mr Postman, look and see — gibt es einen Brief, einen Brief für mich...

Alright, practise: a) write out your phone number in words, in German, b) ask for a one-euro stamp.

Informal Letters

This is the letter-specific stuff you need for KS3 German. Informal letters on this page — that's letters to penpals and friends. It works for postcards too.

Start a letter with "Lieber / Liebe..." — "Dear..."

Use this layout for your informal letters. Town and date on the right, then start and end properly.
Obviously, in a real letter you'd say general stuff about yourself — look through the book, especially sections 2, 3 & 5.

This means 'Dear Karl'. If you're writing to a woman, put *Liebe* instead of *Lieber*.

Put where you live and the date up here. Check out p.3 for dates.

You don't put a capital letter here.

Swansea, den 1. Oktober

Lieber Karl,

vielen Dank für deinen Brief.

Ich habe mich so gefreut, mal wieder von dir zu hören.

Viele Grüße,
Rosa

This means: 'Thanks for your letter.'

These two phrases are really great to use in letters.

This means: 'I was very pleased to hear from you again.'

Best wishes.

Don't panic if you have to write a postcard — just do the same as for a short letter.

Other phrases to use in your letters

Here's a useful phrase you can bung in at the start of any informal letter.
Wie geht's? How are you?

Stick this sentence in just before you sign off.
Schreib bald! Write soon!

This is another way to sign off — you can use it instead of 'Viele Grüße'.
Bis bald. See you soon.

"Bis what?"

What do you call medieval letters — chain mail...

Don't forget it's 'Liebe' for writing to a woman, and 'Lieber' if you're writing to a man. And don't forget a vest. And flippers. And 20p for the phone. And a piece of string and a raisin. Or not.

Formal Letters and Summary Questions

You need a _formal letter_ when you write to book a hotel room, or for writing
to a tourist office in Zurich or something. For more on hotel booking, see p.49.

Learn the special phrases for formal letters

3 things to learn here: 1) The _layout_ (your full address top left); 2) How to _start_; 3) How to _end_.

You _name_ and _full address_ go up here.

Vincent Pilberry
Pilchard Hall
Pilchester
Pilks. PK2 3OS
Großbritannien

Pilchester, den 2.9.2003

Put this if you _don't know_ the person's name.
If you _do_ know, put 'Sehr geehrter Herr Bloggs' or 'Sehr geehrte Frau Blah'.

Sehr geehrte Damen und Herren,

wenn möglich möchte ich bei Ihnen ein Einzelzimmer reservieren, vom 9. bis zum 11. April. Könnten Sie mich bitte informieren wie viel es kosten wird?

"I'd like to reserve a single room at your hotel, from the ninth of April to the eleventh of April."

"Please could you tell me how much it will cost?"

Mit freundlichen Grüßen,

Vincent Pilberry

Vincent Pilberry

Yours sincerely.

Another useful phrase to stick in _just before_ you sign off:

Vielen Dank im Voraus. Thank you in advance.

"For Mal letters"

Use these questions to find out what you've got sussed and what you haven't. Cover up these pages (or else it's cheating) then do all the questions (and no, don't cover the questions). Then go through the pages to check your answers. If you got any wrong, go back and try again.

1) Complete this phrase, in German, writing the numbers out in words: "My telephone number is..."
2) In German, write out how you'd say you want to send a postcard to Scotland.
3) Write a short letter to your Austrian penfriend, Dagmar (a girl). Thank her for her letter, ask her how she is, and tell her to write soon.
4) How do you say "I was very pleased to hear from you again", in German?
5) Write a letter to Mrs Schmidt, asking to reserve a single room from the 1st of May to the 3rd of May. Remember to say "yours sincerely".
6) How do you write "thank you in advance" in German?

Weather and Seasons

This is the <u>question</u> you'll get asked about the weather:

Wie ist das Wetter? = What's the weather like?

Say what the weather's like — "es ist..."

These <u>nine</u> types of weather all start "<u>es ist</u>" ("it is").

 es ist <u>schön</u> it's nice weather

es ist <u>schlecht</u> it's bad weather

 es ist <u>heiß</u> it's hot

es ist <u>kalt</u> it's cold

es ist <u>sonnig</u> it's sunny

es ist <u>wolkig</u> it's cloudy

 es ist <u>windig</u> it's windy

es ist <u>neblig</u> it's foggy

es ist <u>stürmisch</u> it's stormy

ODD ONES OUT

<u>Raining</u> and <u>snowing</u> are <u>different</u>. There's <u>no</u> "ist" in the sentence.

 es regnet it's raining

es schneit it's snowing

The seasons — die Jahreszeiten
['die Jahreszeit' = season]

Ah, the seasons. Only <u>four</u> of them to learn, and <u>two</u> of them are <u>easy</u>. Can't say fairer than that.

 spring

der Sommer summer

der Herbst autumn

 winter

Learn this stuff — or you won't have the neblig-iest...

There's something <u>great</u> about those words for seasons — they're <u>all</u> 'der' words. So why is "Jahreszeit" a "die" word... Ours is not to reason why, but mainly to learn German vocab.

Holidays

Holidays are a bit like weather in a way — they're a good ice-breaker for talking
to people you don't really know. They're also a favourite topic in KS3 German.

Talk about where you normally go on holiday

The bits on the left are the questions you could get asked about holidays.
The bits on the right are your answers — change the underlined bits to match your own holiday.

Wohin fährst du in Urlaub, normalerweise?
Where do you go on holiday normally?

Normalerweise fahre ich nach Schottland.
Normally, I go to Scotland.

For other
countries, see p.50.

Mit wem fährst du in Urlaub?
Who do you go on holiday with?

**Ich fahre mit meiner Mutter
und meiner Schwester.**
I go with my mother and my sister.

*"meiner"
is dative,
see p.59*

For other people,
see p.10.

Wie lange machst du Urlaub?
How long do you go on holiday for?

Ich mache eine Woche Urlaub.
I go for one week.

For other times,
see p.2.

Wo übernachtest du, normalerweise?
Where do you normally stay?

Ich übernachte in einem Hotel.
I stay in a hotel.

*"einem"
is dative,
see p.59*

For other places,
see p.48.

Was machst du?
What do you do?

Ich gehe an den Strand.
I go to the beach.

For other things to
do, see p.35-37.

Wie ist das Wetter normalerweise?
What's the weather like normally?

Es regnet.
It rains.

For other weather,
see p.46.

"A woman watches three men but the
thought bubble above her shows the men
dressed in shirts and ties, revealing that
she is *dressing them* with her eyes." 1950

*When I say they weren't half funny in the
old days, I mean they weren't half funny.*

Oh, I do like to be beside the seaside — so long as it's abroad...

This is a five second RANT WARNING: 5, 4, 3, 2, 1... Don't just learn the answers — you've
GOT TO LEARN THE QUESTIONS TOO. If you don't know the questions you won't be able to
understand what people say to you, and you won't be able to ask them stuff either. ...Rant over.

Hotels and Camping

There are <u>twenty</u> cracking little bits of vocab on this page. Make sure you <u>learn them all</u>.

Learn these <u>places to stay</u>

It's all a question of how much you want to <u>pay</u> per night,
and whether you want <u>ants</u> in your shoes when you wake up.

der Campingplatz
campsite

das Hotel
hotel

die Jugendherberge
youth hostel

At the campsite — <u>auf dem Campingplatz</u>

These are the <u>campsite</u> bits you have to know. Hand-drawn-tastic mate. Watch the <u>spellings</u>, they're <u>odd</u>.

das Zelt
tent

der Wohnwagen
caravan

der Platz
pitch (space for a tent)

der Schlafsack
sleeping bag

das Trinkwasser
drinking water

At the hotel — <u>im Hotel</u>

The most important stuff to learn about hotels is the <u>different types of rooms</u>:

Hotel Rooms

ein Zimmer
room

ein Einzelzimmer
single room

ein Doppelzimmer
double room

Ein Zimmer mit...
A room with

Bad  bath
Dusche shower
Balkon balcony
Badezimmer bathroom
Toilette toilet

Other Stuff

das Telefon
telephone

die Toilette
toilet

der Speisesaal
dining room

der Schlüssel
key

Those tiny shower gel packs make me feel like a giant...

95% of Britons would rather stay in a hotel. 3% are doing their Duke of Edinburgh's Award.
2% have a Ray Mears-complex. 100% of KS3 German students have to <u>learn this vocab</u>.

Booking Accommodation

There's a lot of learning to do on this page. Take it <u>one bit at a time</u> — easy does it.

Booking a <u>hotel room</u> — tell them <u>what</u> and <u>when</u>

Mmm. Booking a room is <u>easier</u> than it seems, just fiddle these phrases to say the <u>dates</u> / <u>number of nights</u> you want. Make sure you read the <u>questions</u> so you'll understand them.

① **Haben Sie Zimmer frei?**   Have you any rooms free?

② *Für wie viele Personen? (For how many people?)*

Ich möchte
I would like

ein Einzelzimmer a single room
ein Doppelzimmer a double room

③ *Für wie viele Nächte? (For how many nights?)*

Ich möchte hier
I would like

eine Nacht one night
zwei Nächte two nights
eine Woche one week
zwei Wochen two weeks

bleiben.
to stay

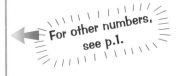
For other numbers, see p.1.

④ *Von wann bis wann möchten Sie bleiben? (When would you like to stay?)*

Ich möchte vom
I would like from the

ersten Juni
first of June
vierten Mai
fourth of May

bis zum
to the

zweiten Juni
second of June
elften Mai
eleventh of May

bleiben.
to stay

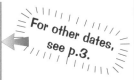
For other dates, see p.3.

*These "first", "second" words are on p.1. Watch out —
they end in "n" in this sentence (it's dative, see p.59)*

⑤ **Was kostet das?**   How much is that?

Ich möchte ein Einzelzimmer. Ich möchte hier eine Woche bleiben,
vom vierten Mai bis zum elften Mai. Was kostet das?

Das kostet €200.

Booking into a <u>campsite</u> — <u>don't</u> ask for a <u>room</u>

The <u>first bit</u> of booking into a <u>campsite</u> is <u>different</u> from a hotel (no rooms in a campsite, see).

① **Haben Sie Plätze frei?**   Have you any pitches free?

② **Ich möchte einen Platz**
I would like a pitch

für ein Zelt for a tent
für einen Wohnwagen for a caravan

...The shower cap makes me feel like my gran...

Write out the whole conversation for getting a room at a hotel. Say you want to stay from 3 July to 6 July. Then write it out <u>again</u>, and keep writing it out till you can do it <u>without</u> looking.

Countries

These are the countries you need for <u>KS3 German</u>. Obviously there are more out there — if you're <u>desperate</u>, look them up in a dictionary, geography-freak. But make sure you <u>learn all these ones first</u>.

Great Britain — <u>Großbritannien</u>

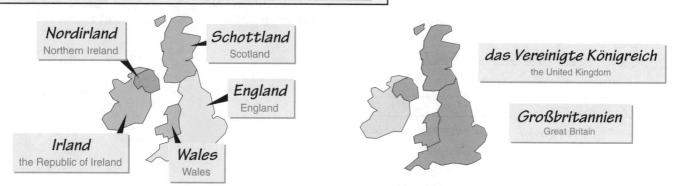

Nordirland
Northern Ireland

Schottland
Scotland

England
England

Irland
the Republic of Ireland

Wales
Wales

das Vereinigte Königreich
the United Kingdom

Großbritannien
Great Britain

The countries of Europe — <u>die Länder von Europa</u>

['das Land' = country]

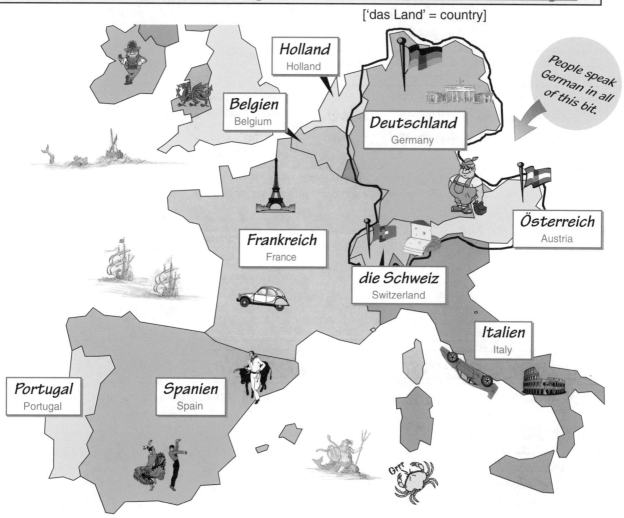

Holland
Holland

Belgien
Belgium

Deutschland
Germany

People speak German in all of this bit.

Österreich
Austria

Frankreich
France

die Schweiz
Switzerland

Italien
Italy

Portugal
Portugal

Spanien
Spain

Grrr

Don't flag — keep going till you've learnt them all...

I reckon "<u>das Vereinigte Königreich</u>" is one of the trickiest phrases in this book, but maybe I've just got a mental block about it... Learn <u>all</u> the countries. You never know when you'll need them.

Nationalities

If someone asks <u>where you're from</u> you can just say "I live in Alaska" — it's "Ich wohne in Alaska".
I've got a strong feeling you'd be talking big, fat, <u>lardy</u> porky pies though.

Saying where you live — "Ich wohne in..."

Pick the one of these that's for where <u>you</u> live, and <u>learn it</u>.

"ich wohne in" + COUNTRY

Ich wohne in England.	Ich wohne in Wales.	Ich wohne in Schottland.	Ich wohne in Nordirland.
I live in England.	I live in Wales.	I live in Scotland.	I live in Northern Ireland.

Saying your nationality — "ich bin..."

This is how you put the sentence together:

"ich bin" + NATIONALITY

Ich bin Engländer. I am English.

You need to learn all the UK nationalities:

Ich bin
I am
- *Engländer(in)* English
- *Waliser(in)* Welsh
- *Nordirländer(in)* Northern Irish
- *Schotte/Schottin* Scottish

They all end with
'in' if you're female

Ich bin Engländer

Ich bin Engländerin

Five foreign nationalities

Five more nationalities that can be tacked on after "Ich bin...":

Salvador Dali

That pic by Leonardo da Vinci

Ronan Keating

Napoleon

Karl Marx

Spanier(in)	**Italiener(in)**	**Ire / Irin**	**Franzose / Französin**	**Deutscher / Deutsche**
Spanish	Italian	Irish	French	German

Ich bin Spanier. Ich bin Enrique Iglesias — honest...

Technically speaking, Napoleon was born on the island of Corsica, so he was <u>Corsican</u>. It's owned
by France though, so you <u>could</u> say he was <u>French</u>. ...But then you wouldn't be able to do <u>great</u>
<u>jokes</u> like: "Can you name Napoleon's nationality?" "Corsican" "Well if you can, go on then." HA HA HA

Summary Questions

Ee, by gum, holidays are grand. No work, no worries, plenty of fun... But the downside of being on holiday is you don't have the honour and privilege of doing KS3 German. Make sure you get everything out of this section — use these questions to check what's sunk in, and what you need to go over again. That means: do the answers once from memory, check what you got right, then doing it again till you get them __all right__. Well worth the effort.

1) Write these weather phrases out in German:
   a) "it's cold"   b) "it's sunny"   c) "it's raining"   d) "it's good weather"

2) Write out what these weather phrases mean in English:
   a) Es ist schlecht.   b) Es ist heiß.   c) Es ist windig.   d) Es schneit.

3) These are three of the seasons. "der Herbst, der Winter, der Sommer".
   What do they mean in English? Write, in German, the name of the missing season.

4) Holidays — how would you say this in German?
   *"Normally, I go to Belgium. I go with my father. I go
   for two weeks. I stay in a youth hostel. I go to the beach."*

5) How do you say these in German?
   a) campsite   b) hotel   c) tent   d) caravan   e) drinking water
   f) single room   g) a room with bathroom   h) dining room

6) Imagine you're trying to book into Hotel Innsbruck. How would you ask if they have any rooms free?

7) How would you say these in German?
   a) I'd like a single room.   b) I would like to stay one week.   c) Which date is it for?

8) What does this mean in English? "Haben Sie Plätze frei?"

9) Write down the four countries of the UK, in German.

10) What are these countries called in English?
    a) Belgien   b) die Schweiz   c) Österreich   d) das Vereinigte Königreich

11) Write these country names out in German: a) France   b) Italy   c) Great Britain

12) Your penfriend Dieter says "Ich wohne in Deutschland. Ich bin Deutscher."
    a) Where does Dieter live? b) What nationality is Dieter? *(not rocket science those ones)*
    c) Write out your own version, to say where you live and what your nationality is.
    d) Write out a version for Brigitte Bardot, who is French and lives in France.

Opinions

There's more than one way to peel a cat... and there's more than one way to <u>say what you think</u>.

"I like" and "I don't like"

Use these four phrases to say what you <u>like</u> and what you <u>don't like</u>.

Ich mag *I like*
Ich liebe *I love*

Ich mag Kaffee. *I like coffee.*
Ich liebe Kaffee. *I love coffee.*

Go orn, naff orf

Ich mag... nicht *I don't like*
Ich hasse... *I hate*

Ich mag Schildkröten <u>nicht</u>. *I don't like tortoises.*
"<u>Nicht</u>" always goes at <u>the end</u> of the sentence.

Ich hasse Schildkröten. *I hate tortoises.*

You can say "I like" using GERN

"<u>Gern</u>" is a handy wee word for saying you <u>like doing something</u>.

1) Write down the <u>verb</u> you want.
(See p.63 for 'what is a verb?')

Ich schwimme gern .
I <u>like</u> swimming.

2) Add <u>gern</u> here — <u>straight after</u> the verb.

Examples:

Ich schlafe gern .
I <u>like</u> sleeping.

Ich esse gern Spaghetti.
I <u>like</u> eating spaghetti.

Use describing words to say what you think

1) Start with the <u>thing</u> you want to describe — a film, a person, a pair of shoes...

2) Then put <u>ist</u> for "is" — or <u>sind</u> for "are".

Kochen ist langweilig.
Cooking is boring.

3) Finish off with a <u>describing word</u>. There are loads more in the box.

gut | good	**leicht** | easy	**super** | super	**lustig** | fun
nicht gut | not good	**schwer** | hard	**wunderbar** | wonderful	**doof** | daft
schlecht | bad	**dumm** | stupid	**toll** | great	**fantastisch** | fantastic
interessant | interesting	**schön** | nice	**anstrengend** | tiring	**einfach Klasse** | totally brilliant

Like it or not German is here to stay...

ARGHH — grammar. Sends a shiver down my spine just to hear the word "<u>grammar</u>".
Don't let it get the better of you. Get a wooden stake and a big bulb of <u>garlic</u> and plough right in.

Asking Questions

Don't sit there like a lump of lard waiting to be <u>asked</u> questions.
Get like Jeremy Paxman — ask questions that make people squirm.

The words have a <u>funny order</u> in questions

Most of the time in German,
the <u>I / you / he / they</u> bit
comes <u>before</u> the verb.

In a <u>question</u> the
verb comes <u>first</u>.

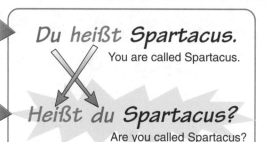

Du heißt Spartacus.
You are called Spartacus.

Heißt du Spartacus?
Are you called Spartacus?

Fig. 167.4: Spartacus begs for mercy, then realises he can see right up Caesar's tunic.

① Make questions by <u>changing the word order</u>

This makes the type of question that gets you a YES or NO answer —
like "Do you like crumpets?" or "Shall we go to the pictures?".
All you do is switch the <u>verb</u> and the <u>I / you / he / they</u> bit, exactly like in the example above.

Englisch ist interessant.   English is interesting

Ist Englisch interessant?   Is English interesting?

Der Hund stinkt.   The dog smells.

Stinkt der Hund?   Does the dog smell?

② Use a question word

1) Start by <u>changing the word order</u>...

2) ...then stick a <u>question word</u>
in at the beginning.

du trinkst ➡ *trinkst du* ➡ *Was trinkst du?*
you are drinking   What are you drinking?

Wo spielst du Tennis?   Where do you play tennis?   *Warum magst du Sonja?*   Why do you like Sonja?

These are the German <u>question words</u> you need to know. They all start with <u>W</u> — a bit like English.

Wer? Who?	*Wo?* Where?	*Wohin?* Where to?	*Wie?* How?
Wann? When?	*Was?* What?	*Warum?* Why?	

This question is for £132,000 — no pressure...

Always, always remember to switch the <u>word order</u>. Oh, and remember the <u>question mark</u> of course. Once you've got those done you can sit and look smug. If you like that kind of thing.

Nouns — Capital Letters & Gender

You need to understand this page, which means you need to know what a <u>noun</u> is:
A noun is a <u>thing</u>, <u>person</u> or <u>place</u>. So "pen", "Julia", "Berlin" <u>are</u> all nouns.
But "sideways" and "big" <u>are not</u> nouns. Ask teach if you're baffled.

Every German noun has a capital letter

In English, only <u>some</u> nouns have a capital e.g. Doris, November, Greenland.
But in <u>German</u>, <u>absolutely every noun</u> has a capital letter. <u>Every single one</u>.

| **Examples:** | Kuli
 (pen) | Zug
 (train) | Hund
 (dog) | Banane
 (banana) | Wahrheit
 (truth) |

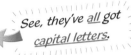

See, they've <u>all</u> got
 <u>capital letters</u>.

Every German noun is masculine, feminine or neuter

Every German noun is either <u>masculine</u>, <u>feminine</u> or <u>neuter</u>. Don't ask me why.

When you're writing, you need to <u>know</u> whether each noun is <u>masc.</u>, <u>fem.</u> or <u>neut.</u> — it affects the <u>words around them</u>. For example, you need different words for "<u>the</u>". Look:

How to say 'the' — der, die and das

In German, there are <u>three</u> words to say "the". *(Sounds weird, but there you go.)*
It's a different word for <u>masculine</u>, <u>feminine</u> or <u>neuter</u>. <u>Plural</u> words are always "<u>die</u>".

The German Words for "THE"

masculine singular	feminine singular	neuter singular	plural (masculine, feminine or neuter)
der	**die**	**das**	**die**

Grammar Fans:
 these are called
 'Definite Articles'.

| **Examples** | <u>der</u> Hund
 the dog
 MASC. | <u>die</u> Katze
 the cat
 FEM. | <u>das</u> Pferd
 the horse
 NEUTER | <u>die</u> Hunde
 the dogs
 PLURAL |

So, it's no good just knowing the German words for things, you have
to know whether each one's <u>masculine</u>, <u>feminine</u> or <u>neuter</u> too.

THE GOLDEN RULE
Each time you <u>learn</u> a <u>word</u>, remember the
<u>der</u>, <u>die</u> or <u>das</u> to go with it — don't think
'dog = Hund', think 'dog = <u>der</u> Hund'.

DER, DIE and DAS
A <u>DER</u> in front
means it's <u>masculine</u>.
<u>DIE</u> in front = <u>feminine</u>.
<u>DAS</u> in front = <u>neuter</u>.

Plurals are tricky

1) <u>English</u> plurals are <u>easy</u> — you usually add an "s"
   (e.g. one boy, two boys).
2) In <u>German</u>, there's <u>no one rule</u> for plurals.
3) There are two things you can do:
   a) *<u>learn each plural off by heart when you learn each word</u>,*
      OR b) *<u>look it up in a dictionary</u>.*

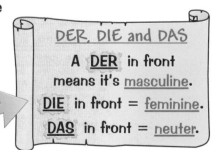

Looking Up Plurals in a Dictionary

1) *Your dictionary might have
   the plural written out, like this:*
   shoe NOUN *der Schuh (PL die Schuhe)*

2) *Or it might have the ending to add
   in brackets:* **shoe** NOUN *der Schuh (e).*

How to Say 'A', & 'My' and 'Your'

Ein means "a", mein means "my". Pretty different, but they have the <u>same endings</u>. <u>Learn 'em together</u>.

How to say "a" — *ein, eine, ein*

1) It's easy in <u>English</u>, there's just one word for "a". You can say "a man", "a woman", whatever.

2) In <u>German</u>, "a" can be "<u>ein</u>" or "<u>eine</u>".
   It depends whether the thing you're talking about is <u>masculine</u>, <u>feminine</u> or <u>neuter</u>.

3) <u>Learn</u> this table <u>off by heart</u>. It's the only way.

The German Words for "A"

masculine singular	feminine singular	neuter singular
ein	**eine**	**ein**

Grammar Fans: these are called '<u>Indefinite Articles</u>'.

Fig 56.1: "A dog", a horse and Austria. Indefinite, traditional dress of Bavaria and Austria.

Examples

<u>ein</u> Hund	<u>eine</u> Katze	<u>ein</u> Pferd
a dog	*a cat*	*a horse*
MASC.	FEM.	NEUTER

My, Your, His, Her — saying whose it is

Grammar Fans: these are called '<u>Possessive Adjectives</u>'.

1) Right. You should be getting the hang of this by now:
   In <u>German</u>, *there is more than one word for "<u>my</u>".*
   It changes to match the thing it's describing — <u>masculine</u>, <u>feminine</u>, <u>neuter</u> or <u>plural</u>.

2) <u>Learn</u> this table. It follows the basic same pattern as "ein" (above).

The German Words for "MY"

masculine singular	feminine singular	neuter singular	plural (masculine, feminine or neuter)
mein	**meine**	**mein**	**meine**

Add an "e" for feminine or plural.

Examples

MASC.	FEM.	NEUTER	PLURAL
<u>mein</u> Hund	<u>meine</u> Katze	<u>mein</u> Pferd	<u>meine</u> Pferde
my dog	*my cat*	*my horse*	*my horses*

3) This is the <u>complete list</u> of the "my", "your", "his" type words.
   They follow the <u>same pattern</u> as "mein" above — you <u>add an "e" for feminine or plural</u>.

The Possessive Adjectives

my:	*mein*	*unser*	:our
your (informal singular):	*dein*	*euer*	:your (informal plural)
his:	*sein*	*Ihr*	:your (formal singular or plural)
her:	*ihr*	*ihr*	:their
its:	*sein*		

Examples

MASC.	FEM.
<u>unser</u> Hund	<u>unsere</u> Katze
our dog	*our cat*

See p.62 for more about this formal/informal stuff.

Be very careful — this stuff is an ein-field...*

"If only German were simpler. If only I lived in a sunny paradise with free biscuits." <u>Knuckle down and get it learned</u>.

*Any similarity to jokes living or dead is purely coincidental. Especially the identical one on p.60.

Pronouns — I, You, He, They...

Pronouns are words that <u>replace nouns</u> — they're words like '<u>you</u>', '<u>she</u>' or '<u>they</u>'.

Frank is playing cards with his dog.
He is about to lose all his money.

'<u>He</u>' is a <u>pronoun</u>. It means you
don't have to say '<u>Frank</u>' again.

I, you, he, she — <u>ich, du, er, sie</u>

Grammar Fans:
these are called
'<u>Subject Pronouns</u>'.

There's no getting round it, you have to <u>learn</u> these little words <u>off by heart</u>.

The Subject Pronouns

I:	*ich*	*wir*	:we
you (informal singular):	*du*	*ihr*	:you (informal plural)
he/it:	*er*	*Sie*	:you (formal singular or plural)
she/it:	*sie*	*sie*	:they
it:	*es*		

See p.62 for more about this formal/informal stuff.

Examples:

1) Daniela and Hans eat bread
   Daniela und Hans essen Brot

   sie essen Brot
   they eat bread

2) Matthias is German
   Matthias ist Deutscher

   er ist Deutscher
   he is German

There are three words for "it" — <u>er, sie</u> and <u>es</u>

Look at that green box above. In German there are <u>three words</u> for "<u>it</u>".
Learn this <u>easy</u> way to remember which word to use — they <u>rhyme</u>:

The 3 "it" Words

"<u>DER</u>" is replaced by "<u>ER</u>".

"<u>DIE</u>" is replaced by "<u>SIE</u>".

"<u>DAS</u>" is replaced by "<u>ES</u>".

Examples:

der Kuli ist rot  *er ist rot*
the pen is red   it is red

die Tür ist rot ➡ *sie ist rot*
the door is red   it is red

das Schloss ist rot ➡ *es ist rot*
the castle is red   it is red

Bet you were ich-ing to learn that — go on then...

It sounds <u>daft</u> in English to say "<u>he</u>" when you mean "<u>she</u>". It's just as <u>daft</u> to mix up things like
"<u>er</u>" and "<u>sie</u>" in German. Learn that <u>green box</u> off by heart, and learn the rules for the <u>3 "it" words</u>.

The Object (a.k.a. When to Use the Accusative Case)

In German you sometimes have to change the <u>endings</u> of words. This page is about changing <u>der</u> and <u>ein</u>.

Sentences can have a <u>SUBJECT</u> and an <u>OBJECT</u>

1) *Every* sentence has a *subject*.

SUBJECT = whoever (or whatever) is <u>doing</u> something

Norma **sang**.

2) Some sentences have an *object* too.

OBJECT = whoever or whatever is <u>having something done to it</u>

Norma **sang a song**.

3) When a word is the object you sometimes have to *change the ending*. Read on...

PICKY RULE 1: Change <u>der</u> to <u>den</u> for the object

1) When a *masculine* word (e.g. *der Wagen*) is the object, change *der* to *den*.

Wagen is the SUBJECT here so leave it as "der Wagen".

Here Wagen is the OBJECT. Change <u>der</u> to <u>den</u>.

(Der) Wagen **ist rot**.
The car is red.

Paul kauft (de**n**) Wagen.
Paul buys the car.

Grammar Fans: 'DEN' is the 'accusative' of DER.

2) *Das* stays the same, for *neuter* words. *Das Hemd ist rot. Paul kauft das Hemd.*
The shirt is red. Paul buys the shirt.

3) *Die* stays the same too, for *feminine* words ...and for *plurals*.

Die Handschuhe sind rot. Paul kauft die Handschuhe.
The gloves are red. Paul buys the gloves.

Die Tomate ist rot. Paul kauft die Tomate.
The tomato is red. Paul buys the tomato.

PICKY RULE 2: Change <u>ein</u> to <u>einen</u>

Grammar Fans: 'EINEN' is the 'accusative' of EIN.

For the OBJECT, change <u>ein</u> before a masculine word to <u>einen</u>.

Paul hat (ein**en**) Wagen.
Paul has a car.

Mein and *kein* have exactly the same endings as *ein* — give them an extra <u>en</u> too.

Er hat (kein**en**) Wagen.
He hasn't got a car.

Er kauft (mein**en**) Wagen.
He's buying my car.

Ein, *mein* and *kein* stay the same for a neuter word.

Paul hat *ein Hemd.*
Paul has a shirt.

Eine, *meine* and *keine* don't change either.

Paul hat *meine Tomate.*
Paul has my tomato.

Objection, your honour — this German's way too hard...

Here it is in a nutshell *(Cue Austin Powers impressions)*: "<u>der</u>" and the other little words that <u>go with</u> "der" words get <u>EN</u> on the end. For "<u>die</u>" and "<u>das</u>" words there's <u>NO CHANGE</u> to the endings.

The Dative Case

Tricky this. Don't blame me. I didn't make you study German and I didn't invent the dative.

Use the DATIVE after these words

The dative's another set of special endings.
You have to put the dative of der, ein, mein and kein after these words:

Grammar Fans: these little words are 'prepositions'.

in = in   *in + dem = im*   **von** = from   *von + dem = vom*

auf = on   **an** = at (place) *or* on (date) *an + dem = am*   **mit** = with

gegenüber = opposite   **zu** = to   *zu + der = zur*
zu + dem = zum

These are the datives for der, ein, mein and kein

These are the datives for der, ein, mein and kein. It's best to just learn them.

	der	die	das	die (pl.)			ein	eine	ein
DATIVE	dem	der	dem	den		DATIVE	einem	einer	einem

	mein	meine	mein	meine (pl.)			kein	keine	kein	keine (pl.)
DATIVE	meinem	meiner	meinem	meinen		DATIVE	keinem	keiner	keinem	keinen

> *You have to make dative plural nouns end in "n" too:*
>
> **meinen Hünden = my dogs (dat.)**

This is how you do it

Say you've got to write "We're playing with my brother" — in German...

1) Write your sentence as far as "mit":

2) Now get the right, dative bit, of mein.
Bruder is a masculine word — so it's meinem.

Wir spielen mit  **meinem Bruder**

3) Put it all together and you get the sentence:

Wir spielen mit meinem Bruder.

We're playing with my brother.

Hmm...

You've got to learn those words at the top of the page so you know when to use the dative.
And when I say "learn" I mean off-by-heart in a slightly freaky saying-it-in-your-sleep kind of way.

Adjectives — Words to Describe Things

Adjectives are those words you use to <u>describe things</u>, like "green", "massive" and "slimy".
You sometimes <u>change the endings</u> in German — it all depends what word comes <u>before</u> the adjective.

The dress IS big — adjectives don't change after "is"

This is the <u>easiest</u> way to use adjectives.
With sentences like this, you stick the adjective in <u>just as it is</u>.

> Grammar Fans:
> yep, these are
> 'adjectives'.

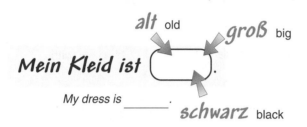

alt old   *groß* big

Mein Kleid ist ⬚ .

My dress is _____ .

schwarz black

*You can use this type
of sentence to give
opinions too — see p.53.*

THE big dress — after der, die and das, ADD E

When the adjective comes after <u>der</u>, <u>die</u> or <u>das</u>, you stick an "<u>e</u>" on the end of the adjective.

der, die, das ➡ *große*

Examples:

der *große* Pulli
the big pullover

die *große* Jacke
the big jacket

das *große* Kleid
the big dress

"Clothes are for wimps."

The adjective goes <u>between</u> the <u>der</u>, <u>die</u> or <u>das</u> and the word you're describing.

A big dress — after ein, the endings are different

Add these endings to the adjective if it comes after <u>ein</u>, <u>eine</u> and <u>ein</u>.

ein ➡ *blauer*

This is what you use
with <u>masculine</u> words.

eine ➡ *blaue*

This is what you use
with <u>feminine</u> words.

ein ➡ *blaues*

This is what you use
with <u>neuter</u> words.

Examples:

ein *blauer* Pulli
a blue pullover

eine *blaue* Jacke
a blue jacket

ein *blaues* Kleid
a blue dress

It's just like with <u>der</u>, <u>die</u> and <u>das</u> — the adjective goes
<u>after</u> the <u>ein</u> or <u>eine</u>, and <u>before</u> the thing you're <u>describing</u>.

Be very careful — this stuff is an ein-field...

Just when you thought adjective-hell was over... How would you say these in German?*
a) The bag is green. *bag=die Tasche*   b) The blue house. *house=das Haus*   c) A black car. *car=der Wagen*

*Answers on page 73.

Making Comparisons

Shall I compare thee to a summer's day? No, best not.
Here's how to say something is "<u>more</u> ...." or ".........<u>er</u>" than something else.

My dress is <u>cheaper</u> — add ER to the adjective

If you need to say something is <u>faster</u>, <u>slower</u>, <u>more grungy</u>, or whatever,
take the basic adjective and add "<u>er</u>":

billig **cheap** + *er* → *billig**er*** = cheap**er** → *Mein Kleid ist billiger.*
My dress is cheaper.

For <u>some words you add an</u> <u>umlaut(¨) and ER</u>

With a few words you don't <u>just</u> stick "<u>er</u>" on the end. You have to add an <u>umlaut</u> too.

kurz **short** → *Kürzer* **shorter**   *groß* **big, tall** → *größer* **bigger, taller**

lang **long** → *länger* **longer**   *alt* **old** → *älter* **older**

> The dictionary will say this:
> **groß** *comp.* (¨)
> *if you need an umlaut.*

You can't just <u>guess</u> which words need an umlaut — learn them as you go along.

Schöner als — nicer than

To compare <u>two</u> things, put <u>als</u> where you'd use <u>than</u> in English.

Your	flat	is	nicer	**than**	my	flat .

Deine Wohnung ist schöner	*als*	*meine Wohnung.*

My tortoise is <u>fastest</u> — add -ste

The German way to say something is "<u>biggest</u>" or "<u>best</u>" is to add <u>-ste</u>.

schnell **fast** → *der/die/das* **Schnell**ste **the fastest** → *schnell**ste*** **fastest** →

der schnellste Zug
the fastest train
er ist der schnellste
it is the fastest

*I looked up "train", I got this.
Look how wet he is. Poor beggar.*

It can be a bit tricky depending on what letters come at the <u>end</u> of the word you're adding to:

groß **big, tall** → *größ**te*** **biggest, tallest**   **You don't need <u>two</u> 's' sounds, so you just add <u>-te</u>.**

interessant **interesting** → *interessant**este*** **most interesting**   **'Interessant<u>ste</u>' would be too hard to say, so you add <u>-este</u>.**

Softer, stronger, and nothing to do with puppies...

A slap in the face with a wet flounder is <u>nicer</u> than a slap in the face with a wet lobster.
But a cooked lobster with plenty of butter and some fresh white bread is <u>nicest</u> of all.

Words for 'You' — 'du', 'Sie' and 'ihr'

In German, there are <u>three words</u> that mean "<u>you</u>". They're "<u>du</u>", "<u>Sie</u>", and "<u>ihr</u>". This page tells you <u>when</u> to use <u>which one</u>. Simple as that.

'du' is for a friend, a family member or a younger person

"<u>du</u>" is the <u>informal</u>, <u>friendly</u> way to say "you" to <u>one person</u>.
Technically, you'd say it's the "informal singular".

① Use '<u>du</u>' for <u>a friend</u> or <u>a close relative</u>

② Use '<u>du</u>' for <u>one person</u> <u>your age</u> or <u>younger</u>

③ Use '<u>du</u>' for <u>an animal</u> or <u>a pet</u>

'ihr' is for two or more friends, family members etc.

"<u>ihr</u>" is the informal <u>friendly</u> way to say "you" to <u>two or more people</u>.
Technically, you'd say it's the "informal plural".

④ '<u>ihr</u>' is like '<u>du</u>', but it's for <u>two or more people</u>

Use 'Sie' for older people and to be polite

"<u>Sie</u>" is the <u>formal</u> way to say "you". It's the same for <u>one</u>, <u>two</u> or <u>more</u> people.
Technically, you'd say it's the "formal singular or plural".

⑤ Use '<u>Sie</u>' to be polite to <u>older people</u> *(who aren't close family or friends)*

EXAMPLES — ASKING PEOPLE HOW OLD THEY ARE:

1) Your dad:
   Wie alt bist <u>du</u>? How old are <u>you</u>?

2) A German kid you've just met:
   Wie alt bist <u>du</u>? How old are <u>you</u>?

3) Your dog:
   Wie alt bist <u>du</u>? How old are <u>you</u>?

4) Two friends:
   Wie alt seid <u>ihr</u>? How old are <u>you</u>?

5) The Queen:
   Wie alt sind <u>Sie</u>?
   How old are <u>you</u>?

Look ihr — du you Sie what I mean...

If you're still having trouble, try learning this <u>flow chart</u>:

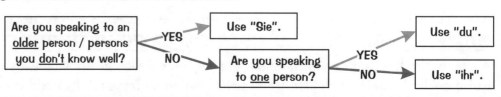

<u>Verbs — Present Tense</u>

Present tense = what <u>is</u> or <u>is happening now</u>. No more chuntering — just get on with it.

<u>Verbs **are** action words — *they tell you* <u>what's going on</u></u>

You need to know what a verb <u>is</u> so you can understand this page. Verbs are "<u>doing</u>" or "<u>being</u>" words.

She <u>eats</u> rice for lunch.

"<u>doing</u>" word

Joe <u>rides</u> to Tibet every day.

I <u>am</u> very happy.

"<u>being</u>" words

Today <u>is</u> a good day.

The <u>present</u> **tense** <u>is</u> *what's happening now*

1) When you look verbs up in a <u>dictionary</u>, it'll give you the "<u>infinitive</u>" form.
For example, machen = to do, kaufen = to buy.

2) To say something in the <u>present tense</u>, you need to <u>change</u> the verb.
For regular verbs take the <u>front part</u> of the verb (without the "<u>en</u>"), and stick on an <u>ending</u>.

3) The <u>endings are the same</u> for all <u>regular verbs</u>. "Machen" is regular, so here it is with its endings...

The first bit ('<u>mach</u>')
doesn't change.

mach<u>en</u> = to do or make

I make =	ich mach **e**	wir mach **en**	= we make
you (informal sing.) make =	du mach **st**	ihr mach **t**	= you (informal plural) make
he makes =	er mach **t**	Sie mach **en**	= you (formal sing & pl) make
she makes =	sie mach **t**	sie mach **en**	= they make
it makes =	es mach **t**		

NOTE: <u>er, sie</u> and <u>es</u> always have the <u>same</u> ending.

Here are some more <u>regular verbs</u> — i.e. these verbs all follow the same pattern as 'machen'. Learn the endings for one and you've learnt them all.

to ask: fragen   *to book:* buchen   *to buy:* kaufen

EXAMPLE

If you want to say something like 'He <u>buys</u> bread', it's dead easy:

Start by <u>knocking off</u> the 'en'.

kaufen

Then <u>add on</u> the <u>new ending</u>.

kauf t

And — <u>ta da</u>...

Er <u>kauft</u> Brot. = He <u>buys</u> bread.

Learn these awkward ones

Learn these awkward ones that <u>don't</u> follow the pattern — they have weird "<u>du</u>" and "<u>er/sie/es</u>" forms.

<u>ess</u>en = to eat			
ich	esse	wir	essen
du	**isst**	ihr	esst
er/sie/es	**isst**	Sie	essen
		sie	essen

<u>seh</u>en = to see			
ich	sehe	wir	sehen
du	**siehst**	ihr	seht
er/sie/es	**sieht**	Sie	sehen
		sie	sehen

<u>fahr</u>en = to go / leave			
ich	fahre	wir	fahren
du	**fährst**	ihr	fahrt
er/sie/es	**fährt**	Sie	fahren
		sie	fahren

<u>les</u>en = to read			
ich	lese	wir	lesen
du	**liest**	ihr	lest
er/sie/es	**liest**	Sie	lesen
		sie	lesen

<u>schlaf</u>en = to sleep			
ich	schlafe	wir	schlafen
du	**schläfst**	ihr	schlaft
er/sie/es	**schläft**	Sie	schlafen
		sie	schlafen

<u>geb</u>en = to give			
ich	gebe	wir	geben
du	**gibst**	ihr	gebt
er/sie/es	**gibt**	Sie	geben
		sie	geben

<u>Get some learning in quick — the ending is nigh...</u>

<u>Crucial</u> stuff this. There's only one way to tackle it — <u>learn</u> that "machen" box like the <u>back of your hand</u>.

Sein, Haben and Separable Verbs

Haben and sein are the two German verbs you need the most.
They don't follow the normal pattern — you just have to learn them off by heart.

The present tense bits of sein and haben are irregular

① 'sein' means 'to be' — it's dead important, but it's also dead weird.

sein = to be

I am =	ich	**bin**	wir	**sind**	= we are
you (informal singular) are =	du	**bist**	ihr	**seid**	= you (informal plural) are
he/she/it is =	er/sie/es	**ist**	Sie	**sind**	= you (formal sing. & plural) are
			sie	**sind**	= they are

② 'haben' means 'to have' — it's the 'hast' and 'hat' bit that don't follow the pattern.

haben = to be

I have =	ich	**habe**	wir	**haben**	= we have
you (informal singular) have =	du	**hast**	ihr	**habt**	= you (informal plural) have
he/she/it has =	er/sie/es	**hat**	Sie	**haben**	= you (formal sing. & plural) have
			sie	**haben**	= they have

Separable verbs can seem confusing, but they're not that hard really. Honest.

Separable verbs are made up of two bits

1) In English, there are loads of verbs made of two bits: EXAMPLES: go out   get up

2) It's similar in German. What's tricky is knowing where the bits go.

> In the infinitive (see top of p.63), they're kind of back-to-front.
>
> EXAMPLES: **ausgehen** = to go out   **aufstehen** = to get up
>   out   go   up   get
>
> When you use them in sentences like "I go out", you split them up,
> and put the first bit right to the end of the sentence.
>
> EXAMPLES: **Ich gehe aus** = I go out   **Ich stehe um fünf Uhr auf** = I get up at five o'clock
>   I   go   out   I   get   at five o'clock   up

3) Here are the other "separable verbs" you need to know. The bit that breaks off is in red.

    abwaschen to wash up   **an**rufen to phone   **ab**fahren to leave
    fernsehen to watch TV   **an**kommen to arrive   **aus**sehen to seem

Irrelevant bit about JFK and the jam doughnut...

In 1963, John F. Kennedy, president of the USA, said in a speech in Berlin, "the proudest boast is Ich bin ein Berliner"
Many people think this was a very funny mistake. They argue that he should've said "ich bin Berliner", which means
I'm a Berliner (i.e. from Berlin), because "ich bin ein Berliner" means "I'm a jam doughnut". Ha ha ha.
*From what I've read on the internet though, 1) a doughnut is only called a "Berliner" in other parts of Germany, 2) he was talking metaphorically,
not literally, and 3) everyone in the audience at the time knew what he meant. But then that'd spoil a good joke. Here's to you, J F Doughnut.*

Modal Verbs

It's handy to have these verbs on one page for <u>three reasons</u>. 1) They're all verbs you <u>use all the time</u>. 2) They're all verbs you <u>use</u> in the <u>same kinda way</u>. 3) They're all a bit <u>weird</u> — you have to learn all the bits.

They're called <u>MODAL</u> verbs because they <u>change</u> ("modify") the meaning of other verbs. Look at how <u>different</u> these sentences are, even though they're all to do with eating:

Ich kann essen.
= I can eat.

Ich will essen.
= I want to eat.

Ich soll essen.
= I should eat.

This is how you use them

You need the <u>right form</u> of the <u>modal verb</u> ("I want" or "he wants") because that's the main verb...

Ich muss *abwaschen* .
= I must wash up.

...and you need the <u>infinitive</u> of the <u>other verb</u> (the basic "en" form). You stick this at the <u>end of the sentence</u>.

<u>können</u> = to be able to / can

I can =	ich **kann**	wir **können**	= we can	
you *(informal sing.)* can =	du **kannst**	ihr **könnt**	= you *(informal plural)* can	
he can =	er **kann**	Sie **können**	= you *(formal sing & pl)* can	
she can =	sie **kann**	sie **können**	= they can	
it can =	es **kann**			

<u>müssen</u> = to have to / must

I must =	ich **muss**	wir **müssen**	= we must	
you *(inf. sing.)* must =	du **musst**	ihr **müsst**	= you *(inf. plu.)* must	
he must =	er **muss**	Sie **müssen**	= you *(formal sing & plu.)* must	
she must =	sie **muss**	sie **müssen**	= they must	
it must =	es **muss**			

<u>dürfen</u> = to be allowed to

I'm allowed =	ich **darf**	wir **dürfen**	= we are allowed	
you *(informal sing.)* are allowed =	du **darfst**	ihr **dürft**	= you *(informal plural)* are allowed	
he is allowed =	er **darf**	Sie **dürfen**	= you *(formal sing & plu.)* are allowed	
she is allowed =	sie **darf**	sie **dürfen**	= they are allowed	
it is allowed =	es **darf**			

<u>wollen</u> = to want

I want =	ich **will**	wir **wollen**	= we want	
you *(inf. sing.)* want =	du **willst**	ihr **wollt**	= you *(inf. plu.)* want	
he wants =	er **will**	Sie **wollen**	= you *(formal sing & plu.)* want	
she wants =	sie **will**	sie **wollen**	= they want	
it wants =	es **will**			

<u>sollen</u> = to be supposed to / should

I should =	ich **soll**	wir **sollen**	= we should	
you *(informal sing.)* should =	du **sollst**	ihr **sollt**	= you *(informal plu.)* should	
he should =	er **soll**	Sie **sollen**	= you *(formal sing & plu.)* should	
she should =	sie **soll**	sie **sollen**	= they should	
it should =	es **soll**			

<u>mögen</u> = to like

I like =	ich **mag**	wir **mögen**	= we like	
you *(inf. sing.)* like =	du **magst**	ihr **mögt**	= you *(inf. plu.)* like	
he likes =	er **mag**	Sie **mögen**	= you *(formal sing & plu.)* like	
she likes =	sie **mag**	sie **mögen**	= they like	
it likes =	es **mag**			

<u>Können the Barbarian?...</u>

Learning six verbs is a <u>pain</u>. Take 'em <u>one at a time</u>. As you do each one, think up some <u>sentences</u> with it in.

Commands and Orders

"Go now", "Get up, get on up", "Stand by me". Yep, pop music's full of commands.
...I'll admit it — you mostly need this stuff for understanding <u>signs</u> and what <u>other people</u> <u>tell you to do</u>.

Tell people what to do...

Grammar Fans:
this is called the
'<u>Imperative</u>'.

1) Giving people <u>orders</u> in German is pretty <u>straightforward</u>.

2) It's basically the <u>present tense</u> (see p.63), <u>fiddled about</u> a bit.

3) Just like the present tense, the <u>way</u> you say an order depends
on <u>who you're talking to</u>. Look at this example for "Go!".

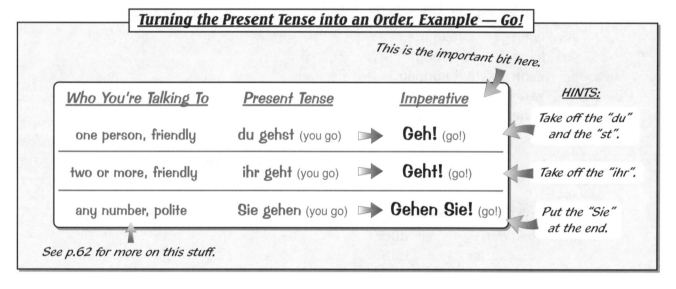

Turning the Present Tense into an Order, Example — Go!

This is the important bit here.

Who You're Talking To	Present Tense	Imperative	HINTS:
one person, friendly	du gehst (you go) ➡	**Geh!** (go!)	*Take off the "du" and the "st".*
two or more, friendly	ihr geht (you go) ➡	**Geht!** (go!)	*Take off the "ihr".*
any number, polite	Sie gehen (you go) ➡	**Gehen Sie!** (go!)	*Put the "Sie" at the end.*

See p.62 for more on this stuff.

4) The key thing is those <u>hints</u> on the right-hand side. Take some time to <u>learn them</u>.

Examples

du kommst (you come) → **Komm!** (Come!)

ihr seid ruhig (you are quiet) → **Seid ruhig!** (Be quiet!)

Sie singen "Ooh, baby" (you sing "Ooh, baby") → **Singen Sie "Ooh, baby"!** (Sing "Ooh, baby"!)

*Ain't got no compost,
ain't got no peat,
Ain't got no shoes
Upon my feet...*

How to tell people what NOT to do

To tell people <u>not</u> to do something, just add "nicht" <u>after</u> the verb for <u>du</u> and <u>ihr</u>.

*See p.69 for
more on <u>nicht</u>.*

Examples   *Geh <u>nicht</u>!* <u>Don't</u> go!   *Seid <u>nicht</u> ruhig!* <u>Don't</u> be quiet!

After <u>Sie</u> the "nicht" goes <u>straight after</u> the <u>Sie</u>.   *Gehen Sie <u>nicht</u>!* <u>Don't</u> go!

Singen Sie "Ooh, baby" nicht — I mean it...

It all boils down to those <u>3 hints</u>, and putting "<u>nicht</u>" on the <u>end</u> for <u>not</u>. Cover up the page, and
write the hints down from <u>memory</u>. If you don't get them <u>100% right</u>, go over it and <u>try again</u>.

Talking About the Past

I wrote this page with a stick and a muddy stone. They didn't have pens in the old days.

The past tense is for talking about the past...

Here's how you make the past tense. There are <u>two</u> important bits.

Grammar Fans: this is called the 'Perfect Tense'.

Ich habe Fußball gespielt . = I played football.

1) You always need a bit to mean "<u>have</u>".

   In <u>English</u>, you don't always need the "have" bit, like in "last week, I played tennis".

   BUT in <u>German</u> you <u>must</u> use the "have" bit.

2) This bit means "<u>played</u>".

   It's a <u>special version</u> of "spielen" (to play).

   In English, most of these words end in "-ed".

There are <u>three parts</u> to getting the perfect tense right:

Past tense part 1 — "haben" (to have)

For the "<u>have</u>" bit of all past tense phrases, you use the <u>present tense</u> of "<u>haben</u>" (see p.64).

Examples

Du hast ein Rad gekauft.
= <u>You have</u> bought a bicycle.

Wir haben ein Rad gekauft.
= <u>We have</u> bought a bicycle.

Past tense part 2 — special past tense words

For all "regular" verbs, you use an easy formula to make the special past tense word.

Formula for the Past Tense Bit

It looks a bit weird — but for <u>regular verbs</u> it's easy.

(1) Add "ge" to the start. (2) Knock off the "en". (3) Add "t" on the end.

 ge ➤ kauf~~en~~ ⬅ t
gekauft

Grammar Fans: the ge-blah bit is called the 'Past Participle'.

These All Follow the Formula

to play:	spielen →	gespielt	:played
to buy:	kaufen →	gekauft	:bought
to make, do:	machen →	gemacht	:done, made
to ask:	fragen →	gefragt	:asked
to say:	sagen →	gesagt	:said
to hear:	hören →	gehört	:heard

Learn these Five Odd Ones Out

to eat:	essen →	gegessen	:eaten
to write:	schreiben →	geschrieben	:written
to see:	sehen →	gesehen	:seen
to drink:	trinken →	getrunken	:drunk

Past tense part 3 — word order

Right, it's a bit strange, but then that's German for you. *The <u>ge-blah</u> word goes <u>at the end</u>.*

Look at the examples on the rest of this page.

That was a great page...

If this stuff seems a nightmare, take a <u>deep breath</u>, <u>relax</u>, and take it <u>one step at a time</u>. Try this: use the page to write "*I have seen a bicycle*", in German. Start from the top, work your way down.

Talking About the Future

You use the <u>future tense</u> to talk about events that are <u>going to happen</u>... in the <u>future</u>.
There are <u>two ways</u> to form the future tense. Start with <u>easy way</u>.

1) Talking about the future — the easy way

Pay attention and enjoy this, it's one of the few occasions I'll give you some really good news:

1) To say that something is <u>going to happen in the future</u>,
   you can just use the <u>normal present tense</u>, and <u>add a time phrase</u>.

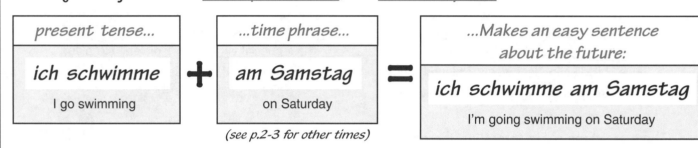

present tense...		...time phrase...		...Makes an easy sentence about the future:
ich schwimme I go swimming	**+**	**am Samstag** on Saturday	**=**	**ich schwimme am Samstag** I'm going swimming on Saturday

(see p.2-3 for other times)

2) The only tricky bit is <u>where</u> to put the <u>time phrase</u>.
   Stick it <u>after the verb</u> (the doing word — see p.63).

Example:

<u>Ich gehe</u> <u>am Dienstag</u> ins Kino. ← "Ich gehe" is the <u>verb</u> bit, so "am Dienstag" goes <u>after it</u>.

<u>I'm going</u> to the cinema <u>on Tuesday</u>.

2) Talking about the future — the harder way

Right, the harder way. This is real higher levels stuff. Only learn this after you've got the easy way completely sussed.

1) In <u>English</u>, you can make the <u>future tense</u> by using "<u>will</u>", and an <u>infinitive</u>. E.g. *He will sing*

2) You can do the <u>same thing</u> in <u>German</u>. For example, *Er wird singen.* (= He will sing)

3) The word for "will" <u>changes</u> to <u>match</u> the <u>person</u> you're talking about.
   You have to choose the right part of "<u>werden</u>". Look at these examples:

werden = will			**Examples:**
I will = ich **werde**	wir **werden** *= we will*		*Ich werde singen.* (= <u>I will</u> sing)
you (informal sing.) will = du **wirst**	ihr **werdet** *= you (informal plural) will*		
he/she/it will = er/sie/es **wird**	Sie **werden** *= you (formal sing & pl) will*		*Wir werden singen.* (= <u>we will</u> sing)
	sie **werden** *= they will*		

4) One last thing — the <u>infinitive</u> always goes at the
   <u>end of the sentence</u>. Look at this example:

Ich werde am Samstag singen. (= <u>I will</u> sing on Saturday)

Ich werde einen tall dark stranger meet...

You'll need to show you can handle the future tense to gain the <u>higher levels</u>. Don't worry if you
make the odd mistake. If you can show that you've generally got the hang of it, you'll be fine.

Negatives — Nicht and Kein

Normally, people'll tell you "ahh, don't be so negative". Not this time, pal. Useful stuff, read on.

A) With a verb, you use "nicht" to say "not"

1) In English you change a sentence to mean the opposite by adding "not".

   EXAMPLE: *I am sporty.* → *I am not sporty.*

2) You can do the same in German — just add "nicht".

   EXAMPLE: *Ich bin sportlich.* → *Ich bin nicht sportlich.*

   = I am sporty.   = I am not sporty.

   Examples

   Ich lese. → *Ich lese nicht.*   *Ich liebe dich.* → *Ich liebe dich nicht.*
   I read.   I don't read.   I love you.   I don't love you.

B) With a noun, you use "kein" to say "not"

1) In English, you can add "no" to make a sentence negative, as in this popular song (all together now...)

   EXAMPLE: *We have bananas.* → *We have no bananas.*

2) It sounds odd in English, but it's normal in German.
    You use "kein" before a noun — it means "no" / "not any".

   EXAMPLE: *Wir haben Bananen.* → *Wir haben keine Bananen.*

   = We have bananas.   "Bananen" is the noun.   = We have not got bananas.
                               The "kein" goes before it.

3) "kein" follows the same rules for endings as "ein".
    For most sentences like this, you need the accusative endings:

Accusative Endings for Kein			
masculine singular	feminine singular	neuter	plural (masculine, feminine or neuter)
keinen	keine	kein	keine

Don't use nicht when you should use kein

The tricky bit is when to use kein and nicht. Remember that nicht means "not", and kein means "not any". Try saying the sentence you're writing in English with "not any" in it. If it makes sense, use kein; if it doesn't, use nicht.

Example

Ich bin nicht sportlich.
   = I am not sporty.

This has to be nicht, because
"I am not any sporty" is rubbish.

Spot the accordion...

Put a cross where you think the accordion
might be. You can have up to five crosses.

Section 8 — Grammar and Phrases

Word Order 1

In German, words don't always come in the same <u>order</u> as you'd in English expect.

Simple sentences are just like English ones

For <u>simple sentences</u> like these ones you can translate <u>word-for-word</u> from English.

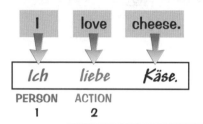

I	love	cheese.
Ich	*liebe*	*Käse.*
PERSON	ACTION	
1	2	

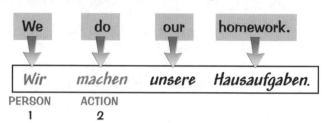

We	do	our	homework.
Wir	*machen*	*unsere*	*Hausaufgaben.*
PERSON	ACTION		
1	2		

START <u>SIMPLE</u> SENTENCES WITH THE <u>PERSON</u>, THEN THE <u>ACTION</u>

You can join up simple sentences — just like in English

1) You can <u>join up</u> simple sentences with these words:

UND = and   **ABER = but**   **ODER = or**

> Grammar Fans: these little words are called 'conjunctions'.

2) Here are two simple sentences with <u>normal</u> word order:

Ich	*bin*	*Berlinerin.*	= I'm from Berlin.
PERSON	ACTION		
1	2		

Ich	*esse*	*nicht Currywurst.*	= I don't eat currywurst.
PERSON	ACTION		
1	2		

3) Join them up using <u>aber</u> and you get:

Ich bin Berlinerin aber ich esse nicht Currywurst.

I'm from Berlin but I don't eat Currywurst.

4) The word order in each chunk of the new sentence stays <u>exactly the same</u> — brilliant.

AFTER <u>UND</u>, <u>ABER</u> AND <u>ODER</u> THE WORD ORDER <u>STAYS THE SAME</u>

If you say WHEN the word order changes

1) In a sentence that says <u>when something happens</u>, put the 'when' word or time phrase <u>first</u>.

Heute	gehe	ich	**wandern.**	= Today I'm going hiking.
TIME	ACTION	PERSON		
1	2	3		

2) The action <u>swaps</u> with the person, so the <u>action</u> comes second, and the <u>person</u> comes third.

3) If there's a phrase with a <u>couple of words</u> for 'when' the whole thing goes first.

Am Montag	**fährst**	**du**	**mit dem Bus.**	= On Monday you're going by bus.
TIME	ACTION	PERSON		
1	2	3		

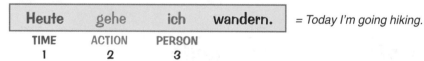

'<u>WHEN</u>' SENTENCES GO: <u>TIME</u>, <u>ACTION</u>, <u>PERSON</u>

Word Order 2

This word order malarkey isn't over yet. This is where <u>joining words</u> (conjunctions) get quite <u>tricky</u>.

These words change the word order <u>two ways</u>

| WEIL = because | WENN = when | OBWOHL = although |

① *In the <u>MIDDLE</u> of a sentence...*

WHEN <u>WEIL</u>, <u>WENN</u> AND <u>OBWOHL</u> COME IN THE <u>MIDDLE</u> OF A SENTENCE, SHUNT THE <u>VERB</u> TO THE <u>END</u>.

<u>Normally</u> "hat" goes here. ↘

But after <u>weil</u> it goes <u>here</u>. ↙

Suzi geht zum Arzt, weil sie Kopfschmerzen hat.

Suzi goes to the doctor's, because she a headache has.

<u>Normally</u> "ist" goes here. ↘

But after <u>obwohl</u> it goes <u>here</u>. ↙

Here's another one: *Vati spielt Golf, obwohl es neblig ist.*

Father plays golf, although it foggy is.

② *At the <u>BEGINNING</u> of a sentence...*

When <u>weil</u>, <u>wenn</u> and <u>obwohl</u> come at the <u>beginning</u> of a sentence they make things seriously tricky. Take this <u>slowly</u>.

Wenn es kalt ist, komme ich mit dem Bus.

When it's cold I come by bus.

You can't cheat at German, you have to learn it. More's the pity...

1) <u>Wenn</u> bumps the verb to the end of this <u>bit</u> of the sentence.

    Wenn es kalt ist,

2) In the next bit of the sentence you <u>swap</u> the ACTION and the PERSON.

Normally it's... *ich komme* ...but after <u>wenn</u> you put... *komme ich mit dem Bus.*

IF <u>WENN</u>, <u>WEIL</u> OR <u>OBWOHL</u> COMES AT THE <u>BEGINNING</u> OF A SENTENCE YOU GET <u>ACTION-COMMA-ACTION</u>

Wenn es kalt <u>ist, komme</u> ich mit dem Bus.

Insert predictable Yoda gag here...

If you think all this switching word order makes learning German a pain, you are <u>not alone</u>.
Let's share our pain. Breathe in... and out. Breathe in... and out. Breathe in... and SCREAM...

Boring But Important Tables

There's <u>nothing new</u> on this page — if you've read the rest of the book you've seen it all before.
It's all a bit boring, but it's <u>so important</u> I've put it in <u>twice</u>.

You've got to know the past, present and future

'Normal' Present Tense
MACHEN — to do, make

singular, informal	I do	ich mache
	you do	du machst
	he/she/it does	er/sie/es macht
plural, informal	we do	wir machen
	you do	ihr macht
plural, formal	you do	Sie machen
	they do	sie machen

'Normal' Past Tense
MACHEN — to do, make

I did	ich habe gemacht
you did	du hast gemacht
he/she/it did	er/sie/es hat gemacht
we did	wir haben gemacht
you did	ihr habt gemacht
you did	Sie haben gemacht
they did	sie haben gemacht

'Normal' Future Tense
WERDEN MACHEN — to be going to do

I will do	ich werde machen
you will do	du wirst machen
he/she/it will do	er/sie/es wird machen
we will do	wir werden machen
you will do	ihr werdet machen
you will do	Sie werden machen
they will do	sie werden machen

N.B. <u>Machen</u> *is a 'normal' regular verb. There are lots of exceptions. Learn them as you go along.*

<u>Sein</u> *is the weirdest of weird verbs.*

SEIN — to be, Present Tense

I am	ich bin
you are	du bist
he/she/it is	er/sie/es ist
we are	wir sind
you are	ihr seid
you are	Sie sind
they are	sie sind

If you get bored, go and play your Alpen horn.

These words are little but dead important

THE — The Definite Article

	MASCULINE	FEMININE	NEUTER	PLURAL
NOMINATIVE (normal)	der	die	das	die
ACCUSATIVE (see P.58)	den	die	das	die
DATIVE (see P.59)	dem	der	dem	den

A — The Indefinite Article

	MASCULINE	FEMININE	NEUTER
NOMINATIVE (normal)	ein	eine	ein
ACCUSATIVE (see P.58)	einen	eine	ein
DATIVE (see P.59)	einem	einer	einem

MY, YOUR, HIS, THEIR
The Possessive Adjectives

		SINGULAR	PLURAL	
singular, informal	my	mein	unser	our
	your	dein	euer	your
	his	sein	Ihr	your
	her	ihr	ihr	their
	its	sein		

plural, informal
plural, formal

<u>The Possessive Adjectives</u> and <u>kein</u> use
<u>exactly</u> the same endings as <u>ein</u>.
(Apart from the plurals, which go NOM: keine, ACC: keine, DAT: keinem.)

What did the table say to the ceiling? — I feel a little flat...

Don't even try and learn everything on this page in one go. If you do you'll probably make your
<u>ears bleed</u>. Get <u>one bit at a time</u> properly <u>soaked</u> into your brain before you go on to the next.

Summary Questions

I admit it — that <u>was</u> the nastiest of nasty sections in this book. But it wouldn't achieve the full bloom of nastiness without some nasty summary questions to top it all off. You know how it works after me banging on for 72 and a bit pages — keep at it till you can answer <u>all</u> the questions <u>without</u> looking back. Only then can you be sure you <u>know your stuff</u>.

1) Translate these sentences into German:
   a) I like cake. b) I love cake. c) I like eating cake. d) Cake is totally brilliant.

2) Write these questions out in German: a) Do you like cats? b) Do you eat cats?
   c) When do you eat cats? d) Why do you eat cats?
   (Katzen = cats; you like = du magst; you eat = du isst)

3) Write all these words out, and give the <u>nouns</u> a capital letter at the beginning:
   tisch   wagen   sein   der   jacke   wenn   haus   hunger   fußball   tragen

4) Are these <u>masculine</u>, <u>feminine</u>, or <u>neuter</u>? a) der Tisch   b) die Küche   c) das Sofa

5) Write all these out in German *(violin = die Geige)*: a) a violin b) my violin c) his violin
   d) their violin   e) your violin *(informal, singular)*   f) your violin *(informal, plural)*

6) Rewrite these sentences, with *er, sie, es* or *wir* instead of the names of the people or things.
   a) Liese und Lotte reden.   b) Die Katze isst.   c) Ich spiele Klavier mit Anton.

7) Fill the gaps in these sentences with *der, die, das* or *den.*
   a) _____ schnellste Pferd hat gewonnen. b) Der Vogel kauft _____ Pferd.
   c) Das Pferd liebt _____ Vogel. d) _____ Katze hasst _____ Mäuse.

8) Use each of these words once to fill in the gaps: *einen   mein   keinen*
   a) *My car goes slowly.* _____ Wagen fährt langsam.
   b) *Have you got a guitar?* Haben Sie _____ Gitarre?
   c) *I haven't got a cauliflower today.* Heute habe ich _____ Blumenkohl.

9) Choose the right word to fill the gap in each sentence.
   a) der / die / das / dem   *Ich sitze auf _____ Tisch.*
   b) ein / eine / einem   *Ich wohne gegenüber _____ Park.*
   c) mein / meine / meiner   *Du spielst mit _____ Schwester.*

10) Translate these phrases into German: a) the big rabbit b) a small dog c) a small cat

11) Translate these into German:
    a) The rabbit is bigger. b) The rabbit is bigger than the dog.
    c) The cat is smaller than the dog.   d) The rabbit is the biggest.

12) To say "you" to these people, would you say "du", "Sie" or "ihr"?
    a) your mum   b) your mate's annoying little brother
    c) everyone else in your class   d) your head teacher (to his/her face)

13) Translate these into German: a) you *(singular, informal)* are drinking *(trinken)*
    b) you *(singular, informal)* are sleeping *(schlafen)* c) we are (sein)

14) Translate these into German: a) He phones at four o'clock. b) Today I am washing up.

15) (For a change) stick these into German: a) I should go. b) She likes cheese.

16) What do these mean in English? a) Schwimm! b) Essen Sie! c) Komm!

17) Put the missing bit of *haben* in to make these sentences past tense, and translate them:
    a) *Ich _____ geschrieben.* b) *Wir_____ gehört.* c) *Ihr _____ gefragt.*

18) Put the missing bit of *werden* in to make these sentences future tense, and translate them:
    a) *Du _____ spielen.* b) *Sie* (she) *_____ essen.* c) *Ihr _____ sehen.*

ANSWERS (from p.60): a) Die Tasche ist grün. b) Das blaue Haus. c) Ein schwarzer Wagen

Index

There wasn't room to put every last word from the book in here.
If you can't find the word you want try looking under something more <u>general</u>.
e.g. If you can't find "<u>January</u>" look under "<u>months</u>". If you can't find "<u>tortoise</u>" look under "<u>pets</u>".

Index

Index

If you can't find the word you want try looking under something more general.
e.g. If you can't find "January" look under "months". If you can't find "tortoise" look under "pets".